Traffic And Conversion Mastery

By

C. Mike Lewis

and

A Dozen Marketing Experts

Copyright © 2016

Published by BrandedExpertPublishing.com

ISBN-13: 978-1523609703

ISBN-10:1523609702

Legal Disclaimer

All Rights Reserved. No part of this publication may be reproduced in any form or by any means, including scanning, photocopying, or otherwise without prior written permission of the copyright holder.

Disclaimer and Terms of Use: The Authors and Publisher have strived to be as accurate and complete as possible in the creation of this book, notwithstanding the fact that they do not warrant or represent at any time that the contents within are accurate due to the rapidly changing nature of the Internet. While all attempts have been made to verify information provided in this publication, the Authors and Publisher assume no responsibility for errors, omissions, or contrary interpretation of the subject matter herein. Any perceived slights of specific persons, peoples, or organizations are unintentional. In practical advice books, like anything else in life, there are no guarantees of income made. Readers are cautioned to rely on their own judgment about their individual circumstances to act accordingly. This book is not intended for use as a source of legal, business, accounting or financial advice. All readers are advised to seek services of competent professionals in the legal, business, accounting, and finance fields.

Table of Contents

Forward v

Chapter 1: Cory Michael Sanchez
Cash Is King.. 1

Chapter 2: Ira Rosen
My Credit Score?... 13

Chapter 3: Tom Cone
Leveraging the Resources of MemberGate 23

Chapter 4: Jason Myers
Quit Doing It Wrong! 33

Chapter 5: Mike Hill
Vetting For Yourself and Your Business 41

Chapter 6: Daven Michaels
Mentorship, Masterminding and Coaching 53

Chapter 7: Tom Beal
10X Your Business in 22 Minutes 67

Chapter 8 : Lou Brown
Put Your Trust In Me 75

Chapter 9: Steve Sipress
The WOW! Strategy™.. 83

Chapter 10: Matt Bacak
The Case Against Making A Windfall of Money 95

Chapter 11: Sheila Farragher-Gemma
Sponsoring A Successful Event 101

Chapter 11: Carolyn Lewis
Become A Branded Expert and Show Your AUTHORity 111

Chapter 12: C. Mike Lewis
Membership Has Its Privileges 121

"An investment in knowledge pays the best interest"

~Benjamin Franklin~

Foreword

"What really knocks me out is a book that, when you're all done reading it, you wish the author that wrote it was a terrific friend of yours and you could call him up on the phone whenever you felt like it. That doesn't happen much, though."
— *J.D. Salinger, The Catcher in the Rye*

Unless you're part of Traffic and Conversion!

Inside this book you will find some of the most brilliant minds sharing their secrets for success. Each author is a good friend, whether old or new, and always ready, willing and able to help other entrepreneurs to best their business.

We have been honored to have an eclectic group of powerhouses share their insights and expertise with their peers. So take the time to read and re-read these amazing stories. If you find yourself in need of a friend or mentor, reach out to find out not only how we can help take your business to the next level, but how you, too, can help us.

Yes, J.D., we *can* call our authors friends!

Carolyn Lewis

"The Book Diva"

> *"You must gain control over your money or the lack of it will forever control you."*
>
> *~Dave Ramsey~*

Traffic and Conversion Mastery

Chapter One

Cash is King

By Cory Michael Sanchez

Being an Entrepreneur means making a difference. It means helping the economy, providing jobs, and changing lives. But who's helping the Entrepreneur get the funding they need?

Forbes recently reported that Entrepreneurialism is at an "all time high" in an article by Elaine Pofeldt entitled *U.S. Entrepreneurship Hits Record High*. (www.forbes.com/sites/elainepofeldt/2013/05/27/u-s-entrepreneurship-hits-record-high/)

There's one thing that separates a healthy company from the next "out of business" statistic. And that's cold hard cash.

You see, without it, businesses go the way of the dinosaur faster than you can say the word "bankrupt." With it, they thrive and go on to get bigger and bigger.

Most entrepreneurs know that there is a dramatic need for businesses to have a healthy cash flow and always have sufficient funds on hand in order to stabilize and grow their business. Without it a business can die.

Ever felt the pressure of having only a few dollars in your bank account?

Isn't it excruciating? It makes you feel powerless, desperate.

Like the world is crashing in around you and there's nowhere to turn.

After all, there are people who depend on you. Your family. Your employees. You.

The good news is... there is hope.

Traffic and Conversion Mastery

It's time for all your money challenges to change for the better.

- It's time that you can make the investments in your company that will skyrocket your company to new heights.
- It's time that you can purchase the vital equipment you need to scale your business, to have the funds for marketing and advertising so you can scale your business.
- It's time you got the working capital that you need to finally realize your dreams.

And it all starts here.

You see, we were in your spot. And then we learned how to get lifesaving funding for our business.

It was like the whole world opened up to us. We were no long a prisoner in our own business. We finally had the resources to take it to the next level.

And we want the same for you.

We took little known methods of funding and put them all into the ultimate funding book that shows you safe and effective ways to get funded.

Sit back and enjoy as your financial concerns become a "thing of the past."

Making It Rain!

When your business is properly funded you can invest money in the areas needed to spur growth. What would you fund immediately if you had the money?

- **Buy Inventory.**
    - Purchase the inventory you need to be competitive.
        - Receive quantity discounts.

- Purchase against future cost increases.
- Keep "buffer" stock on hand due to the uncertainty of demand and lead time.
- Increase sales by offering an expanded inventory. This allows your customers to purchase related items from you in addition to those they normally buy from you.

- **Invest in Infrastructure.**
  - Purchase new equipment for your business.
    - Increase efficiency and quality.
    - Add more services/products.
    - Improve workplace safety.
    - Gain access to vendor support and warranties.
    - Increase security.
    - Take advantage of tax incentives.
  - Add more employees because you have the infrastructure to support them.

- **Increase Market Share and Acquire New Customers** by increasing your marketing, advertising and promotion budget.
  - As you increase your advertising and marketing budget you'll capture a larger share of your market.
  - Increase your exposure to potential new clients and retain current ones.
  - Sales will increase because everybody likes to work with the winning team.
  - Reach out to existing and potential customers through press releases, newsletters and social media that promote your growth.

- **Payroll.**
  - A well-staffed business allows its owners to pursue growth rather than be distracted by completing tasks that others can accomplish for them.
  - Hire new, qualified employees to help streamline processes, suggest new ones and increase your companies' ability to perform

quality work.
- Take the pressure off of existing employees to increase retention.

- **Hire Freelancers.**
  - Freelancers help you complete projects or perform specialty work such as accounting or marketing, freeing your time for other revenue generating activities.

- **Improve Your Reputation.**
  - As potential customers see you promoting your company and its services and products, they will view you as a successful business with a good reputation.
  - Purchase Reputation Management Software so you always know the reviews and comments people are making about your company. Negative comments can be resolved quickly before they get out of hand.

- **Purchase Real Estate.**
  - Buying a building rather than leasing offices allows you to build an asset that can appreciate in value.
  - Lease office space in your purchased building to add an additional income stream to your businesses.
  - "Tax free cash flow. It's no secret that because of depreciation and mortgage interest deductions (if you leverage your capital), your cash flow should be tax-free. That's right! The far majority of the time an investor will never pay taxes on their cash flow and can wait for capital gains on the sale of the property in the future" according to an article in Entrepreneur titled *Why You Should Be Investing Your Money In Real Estate* written by Mark J. Kohler, Esq., CPA
    http://www.entrepreneur.com/author/mark-j-kohler

- **Add a Franchise.**
  - Buying into a franchise is less risky than a straight start up as it allows you to leverage existing brand awareness,

infrastructure and systems that will allow you to focus on much more rapid growth.
- **Acquire Competition.**
    - By purchasing competitors, you can immediately acquire new customers and immediately grow your business.
    - Buying companies with similar products and services eliminates them from the competition pool.

Picture yourself in a situation where you have everything that you need to sustain and expand your business. This means something different to each of us. For you it may mean enough stock to fill all of your orders, computers that work, new software to help manage inventory, a phone system that's easy to use, the next generation of machinery, or highly qualified employees who have your back.

This can be you if you act to fund your dreams. Remember that if you do the same old things you will get the same old results. Choose to do something that your future self will thank you for.

Where Did All The Funding Go?

Have you ever been turned down by a bank for financing?

If you haven't it's only a matter of time before you feel the cold grip of rejection from the antiquated and out dated banking system. But relax, being turned down by a bank is the rule, not the exception.

Ever notice that banks want to give you money only when you don't need it? It's like giving you an umbrella when the sun is shining.

If you do go the route of traditional bank financing, there's a "boat load" of paperwork and stringent requirements including: Good business credit, great financials, assets to secure the loan, a phenomenal business plan, and a minimum number of years in business. With those qualification standards, only a tiny sliver of small businesses actually qualify.

If you're like most businesses, then you realize that bank financing is not likely to yield the results you are looking for...leaving you without the financial "leg up" that you need.

It's time to look at other viable options...

Crowdfunding
You've probably heard about crowdfunding – maybe you've even looked into it. Here are some of the popular sites and what they say about themselves.

- Indiegogo
    - Helps individuals, groups and non-profits raise money online to make their ideas a reality.
- Krowdster
    - The first crowdfunding marketing platform, designed to optimize and promote rewards and equity crowdfunding campaigns.
- CircleUp
    - A leader in equity-based crowdfunding, CircleUp focuses on angel investments in consumer products companies.
- Kickstarter
    - The world's largest funding platform for creative projects. A home for film, music, theater, games, comics, photography, art, design, and more.

How Crowdfunding Works

After you choose your platform, you post a description of your project, product or service, an outline of your business plan, the amount of capital you are seeking and an explanation of what your contributors will receive in return.

Crowdfunding from Indiegogo, Krowdster, CircleUp, Kickstarter, and others lets businesses pool small investments from lots of different investors.

Like anything else in business, crowdfunding should be approached with caution. The problem is too many people rush in without really knowing what's at stake.

What seems like a great opportunity, turns out to be a nightmare. In fact, it's not hard to wind up with nothing from crowdfunding.

One of the problems with crowdfunding that you should know about before you get involved is that you could set a goal to raise $5,000, pull in $4,900, and then get zero funding because you're a $100 short.

If you want to hit up your brother for the last hundred, that's fine, but you might not even get the chance to, because it's too late.

Types of Crowdfunding

When making your offer on a crowdfunding platform you are hoping that individuals will support your cause or business. There are 2 types of crowdfunding:

One is donation based, meaning that the money is given to you in exchange for a product or service gift. As example, if you are crowdfunding for a new cold food storage container you invented your investors would expect to receive the container in return for their investment.

Equity crowdfunding takes this same concept but instead of expecting a gift, individuals invest for an eventual financial return in the business. As of 2012 and thanks to the JOBS Act, companies are allowed to collect up to $1 million per year over the Internet, so with this type of crowdfunding those who contribute could become company shareholders.

Pros of Crowdfunding
- You don't necessarily have to be a great public speaker or create fancy presentations as in the past when you went directly to Venture Capitalists to obtain funding.
- You have a much broader audience for your offer and along with social media you can easily spread your message.

Cons of Crowdfunding
- Research shows that smaller funds are easier to attain than larger ones.
- If you need money fast you may not receive it when you wish to have it. It's not possible to know in advance how much time it'll take to raise the funds you need.
- Equity crowdfunding investors normally want a fast return on their money and a lawsuit could occur if this doesn't happen.
- If you do not meet your fundraising goal, all of the money that was committed to your project is returned to the investors.

There can be so many variables but it's absolutely a viable method of getting the funding that you need.

Now, let's show you a brand new funding model that is sweeping the nation.

New Funding Phenomenon: Credit Access Funding

What would you do first if you obtained the sum of money that you've desired for a long time?

How would your life change if you received the money in as little as 2 weeks?

Traffic and Conversion Mastery

Where would your business be in 6 months if you were able to fund all of the projects that you know would help it grow?

Dream for a moment.

Your wish is now possible with a brand new class of funding that is helping businesses all over the country make their dreams come true.

It's called "Signature Lines of Credit."

It's a loan based on your credit history and signature. These products are also referred to as personal loans, unsecured loans or character loans.

Signature loans are becoming extremely popular right now because they can be the easiest and simplest way to get funded.

Interest rates depend on the applicant's credit score. MojoFinancial.com offers a credit restoration program to help you obtain the lowest APR possible.

Benefits of signature loans include:
- You don't need to put up any collateral.
    - Such as a car title or property
- You don't need a co-signer.
- The rates are usually better than those of credit cards.
- Adding a signature loan to a mix of responsible credit payments can increase your credit score.
- You receive a lump sum of cash without the "cash advance" fee typically charged by credit cards.
- You get your money quickly.

- In as little as 2 weeks' time. If your credit needs to be repaired it will take longer.
- Repayment time limits are usually flexible.

Best of all, you can spend the money on whatever you want.

Folks usually have some questions or comments around this type of funding:

- I don't have good credit so I can't get a loan.
  - We offer a proven process to fix your credit scores. You can't be funded in 2 weeks, but we will teach you what you need to do to get funded.
- I don't have a business.
  - You don't need one to get funded.
- I wouldn't know what to invest the money in.
  - We help you by offering advice from Veteran Business Owners on the best investments they have ever made for their business.
- I need money right away.
  - Some methods show you how to get funded in as little as two weeks.
- I need a lot of money!
  - There are funding options up to the millions of dollars. It's up to you how much money you go after.
- I'm lazy. This doesn't take work does it?
  - Some methods take almost no work at all.
- This sounds to be good to be true. I'm scared.
  - We offer proven methods that are both safe and secure.

MojoFinancial.com unlocked the key to free you from these fears. We'll show you how to get properly funded using proven methods.

About Cory Michael Sanchez

Winner of "Marketer of the Year" Award through the Phoenix Business Journal, Cory Michael Sanchez is considered one of the top and most respected experts in the Financial and investment arena, LinkedIn lead generation and Video Marketing globally. Author of 4 other highly acclaimed books, including *LinkedIn for Leads*, *"Got Mojo?" 6 Award Winning Secrets for Explosive Business Growth* and *Zero to Hero*, he is the co-founder, pioneer and technical visionary behind Mojo Global's success.

As chief architect of Mojo's award winning softwares and powerful information products, he has dedicated his life to doubling, tripling, and quadrupling profitability in businesses through automation.

Cory Michael Sanchez has trained tens of thousands of entrepreneurs in over 30 countries on how to attract high paying prospects, create a following of raving fans, and easily close lucrative deals.

Host of The Mojo Marketing Edge and the Video Marketing Expert Series, he has interviewed hundreds of elite level guests such as Mike Filsaime, Andy Jenkins, Brad Fallon, Les Brown, Mark Victor Hanson, Joe Polish, and other business legends.

Cory Michael Sanchez was a national champion gymnast at Arizona State University. A scientist in a previous life, he holds a degree in Molecular Biosciences & Biotechnology from ASU and resides in Scottsdale, Arizona.

To learn more about how Cory can help you take your business to the next level, visit him at

http://mojoglobal.com and http://mojofinancial.com

Chapter 2

My Credit Score?

By Ira Rosen

Most of us already know that it's important to maintain a great credit and some of us lost our good credit during the great recession. In this chapter we'll look at some of the many areas of our daily life which can be affected by our credit score and more important what we can do about it.

How Credit Scores are Determined

According to FINRA's website (Financial Industry Regulatory Authority) in an article entitled *How Your Credit Score Impacts Your Financial Future*, "The most well-known credit scoring system was developed by Fair Isaac Corporation and is called the FICO® score. The three major credit bureaus—Equifax®, TransUnion® and Experian®—use the FICO scoring model for their proprietary systems.

Since each scoring system uses a slightly different statistical model, your score from each of the three will not be exactly the same. This is because lenders and other businesses report information to the credit reporting agencies in different ways, and the agencies may present that information through their proprietary systems differently." Visit www.FINRA.com for more information.

Credit Score Ranking

According to Credit.com "...Most credit scores...operate within the range of 301 to 850. Within that range, there are different categories, from bad to excellent.

- Excellent Credit: 750+
- Good Credit: 700-749

- Fair Credit: 650-699
- Poor Credit: 600-649
- Bad Credit: below 600

But even these aren't set in stone. That's because lenders all have their own definitions of what is a good credit score. One lender that is looking to approve more borrowers might approve applicants with credit scores of 680 or higher. Another might be more selective and only approve those with scores of 750 or higher. Or both lenders might offer credit to anyone with a score of at least 650, but charge consumers with scores below 700 a higher interest rate!" states Credit.com on its website."

FINRA created a table that shows what components factor into your score and how much weight is attributed to each one:

Component	Component Weight
Payment history	35%
How much you owe	30%
Length of credit history	15%
Type of credit	10%
New credit (inquiries)	10%

In addition, knowing your FICO® Score is important since it also affects credit and lending decisions. Your score is based on your credit report, so having accurate reporting from all 3 bureaus is imperative.

"The FICO® Score rank-orders consumers by how likely they are to pay their credit obligations as agreed. The latest US version, FICO® Score of 9 is the most current and predictive FICO® Score" according to FICO's website at www.FICO.com.

Which Types of Purchases and Decisions are Influenced by Credit Scores

Here is a quick list of the things that are impacted by credit. Poor credit may result in having to pay higher interest, being required to have a co-signer for a loan, or needing to put down a deposit.

- Auto Loans
- Cell Phones
- Child Support Enforcement Agencies
- Banks
- Business Loans
- Employers
- Insurance
- Mortgages
- Private Student Loans
- Utility Accounts

An Example of How Much Money You Can Save by Having Good Credit

"Suppose you want to borrow $200,000 in the form of a fixed rate thirty-year mortgage. If your credit score is in the highest category, 760-850, a lender might charge you 3.307 percent interest for the loan 1. This means a monthly payment of $877. If, however, your credit score is in a lower range, 620-639 for example, lenders might charge you 4.869 percent that would result in a $1,061 monthly payment. Although quite respectable, the lower credit score would cost you $184 a month more for your mortgage. Over the life of the loan, you would be paying $66,343 more than if you had the best credit score. Think about what you could do with that extra $184 per month." Visit FINRA for more information at:

www.finra.org/investors/how-your-credit-score-impacts-your-financial-future#sthash.6vfEQQbo.uyoKxzpV.dpuf

Factors that Can Help and/or Hurt Credit Scores

- Payment History
    - How you pay your credit cards, retail accounts, installment loans, finance company accounts and mortgages affects your credit score. Understandably, prompt payment helps improve your score, late payments hurt your score.
- Amounts Owed
    - High outstanding balances will hurt you.
    - Paying down an installment loan will help you.
- Length of Your Credit History
    - The longer you have shown good credit management the higher your credit score will be.
- What Kinds Of Credit You Have Taken Out
    - Examples of this are taking credit out to finance the purchase of a boat (not a necessity) which may hurt your credit.
- Credit Inquires
    - When someone has multiple credit inquires it suggests to the credit bureau that you may take on more debt which can lower your score. These type of inquiries are called "hard" hit/inquiries
    - For example, if you are looking

- To purchase furniture and try to obtain credit cards from multiple stores in a short time period your credit may suffer because each inquiry is considered a "hard" hit/inquiry by the credit agencies.
- Conversely, if you are looking for the best available mortgage or car loan rates, and you make multiple inquires within a 14-day period you will only get dinged for 1 "hard" hit/inquiry since it's presupposed by the credit bureau that you'll only be taking out 1 loan.
  - Another type of credit inquiry is called a "soft hit."
    - Soft hits include requests from you to get a copy of your credit report, requests from lenders to give you "pre-approved" credit offers and those that come from potential employers. Soft hits will not affect your credit score positively or negatively.

According to a recent study by the Federal Trade Commission, "**One of every five American consumers has an error on his or her credit report** and 5 percent of us endure errors so serious that we likely are being overcharged for credit card debts, auto loans, insurance policies and other financial obligations, according to a comprehensive study issued..." www.creditcards.com/credit-card-news/ftc-credit-report-mistakes-1270.php#ixzz3vrwTxP2s

A Cautionary Tale

In December, 2015 Huff Post Business reran an article entitled *It's Disturbingly Likely That Your Credit Report Is Wrong* which showcases the consequences of credit reporting gone wrong:

"Jeffrey Beaubien likes to review his credit score on his birthday every year. The 47-year-old father of two has good reason to stay on top of his credit rating. In 2012, he says, he found out that the three biggest credit bureaus in the country had made a whopping mistake on his credit reports: They were each reporting that he was liable for roughly $77,000 more of his son's student loans than he should have been. "I was livid when I found out," said Beaubien, who lives in Eden Prairie, Minnesota.

What made him even more livid, he says, were the consequences of the credit bureaus' mistake. Beaubien says when he got a car loan in 2011, he had to pay a 17 percent interest rate. The next year, he says, he was denied a home loan. Both were a result of his reported debt-to-income ratio being so high."

Common Credit Errors to Look For

- Late payments that are more than 7 years old
- Credit Cards or Loan Accounts that aren't yours
- Accounts that you closed but are listed as closed by the provider
- A paid-off collections account that is still showing as unpaid
- A paid tax lien that's more than 7 years past the date of the payment
- An account that was discharged in bankruptcy but is still showing up as active
- Wrong names
- Wrong addresses
- Inaccurate employer information

Although it's possible to dispute the individual items that make up your credit history it can be a long and tedious process. You must contact and work with each of the 3 agencies directly who will in turn work with each of your creditors.

The great news is MOJO has created a **"Done for You" Credit Restoration Option** that leaves all of the paperwork and follow up to us. Because the focus of one of our teams is solely to improve your credit we usually take much less time than someone who is doing this on their own.

One of MOJO's friends had Steller credit. That is until she went through a divorce and discovered that her ex-husband had trashed it. It took over 2 years for her to go from Poor to Very Good credit, and her credit bureau reports still contain errors.

When we told her that another friend of MOJO had gone from a credit score in the 500's to over a 700 in a span of 2 months using the MOJO Done for You Credit Restoration Option she said she wished she had known about our program years earlier!

Next Steps

Cash for funding business is as necessary as oxygen to our bodies. The more funding you have the more you can scale your business and leverage opportunities that come your way.

Today's new financial landscape offers Small Businesses and Entrepreneurs access to new sources of fast and safe funding.

Stop Worrying About

- Your Credit
- Your Financial Statement
- The Mysteries Of Finance

Stop

- Wasting Time Waiting For A Yes or No
- Chasing Dreams

- Hitting Dead Ends
- Wasting Time Filling Out Forms

Don't waste time like we did.

- Learn from our mistakes
- Profit from our contacts
- Use our proven approach

Remember, you can never have too much money because everything is cyclical, and you always want to be prepared for tomorrow's eventualities.

Take the next step.

Set up an appointment to meet with one of our advisors. Get your business the money it needs...get The Ultimate Funding Formula right now.

About Ira Rosen

Ira Rosen has successfully created, run and sold numerous multi-million dollar companies. At age 30 he was a pioneer in auto leasing and the country's youngest new car auto dealer with multiple franchises. He has also had one of the most successful medical weight loss clinics in the entire country employing doctors, fitness trainers, nurses, dietitians, and psychologists in the mid-90's. During this time Ira and his elite medical team successfully treated and empowered over 10,000 patients. Over the years Ira has acted as a trusted advisor to executives in the board room as well as two 18 year old entrepreneurs who had $20, a dream, and a business plan on the back of a napkin. Ira has proven to be a nationally recognized as an innovative marketing strategist, pioneering numerous complicated creative break-through market solutions.

Ira has been an avid running enthusiast his entire life. He has run numerous marathons around the country. Most recently Ira ran the P.F. Chang with his two daughters. Ira started running at age 15 and has logged over 100,000 miles (once around the earth is 25,000 miles) and he is currently working on his 5th lap.

To learn more about how Ira can help you and your business, visit him at **http://mojoglobal.com**

> *"Twenty years from now you will be more disappointed by the things that you didn't do than by the ones you did do."*
>
> *~Mark Twain~*

Chapter 3

Leveraging the Resources of MemberGate

By Tom Cone

To talk about the opportunities of running an online subscription business, let me take you back to the late 90s, when the World Wide Web was first was coming out...

I was working for the UK government helping rural businesses in Yorkshire, who were hit hard by an outbreak of Foot and Mouth Disease. My role was to stimulate trade, create new opportunities for businesses to flourish and help farmers diversify.

Rural businesses such as farms, restaurants, B & B's, retailers, manufacturers, etc. face the same challenges, same headaches and same marketing problems as urban businesses, except they have less local customers to trade with.

This was a time when businesses were taking their 8 page brochures and converting them to 8 page web-sites. It was a time when Desktop Publishing was suddenly available and every business had a newsletter they needed to post out!

At that time nobody knew anything about how to this thing called the World Wide Web, so I flew over to the USA and took several workshops and courses with leading marketers like Bill Myers and Jay Abrahams.

When I came back to England I was all geared up to do all kinds of clever stuff, but couldn't. Back home, businesses hadn't even registered their domain names, never mind web sites and email!

So to solve this I launched a "done for you" web-site service using a software package called eShowcase, helping people get started with their first website

Then I ran my own workshops and seminars on how to make the most of the internet, how to build a better website, how get more customers from the web, how to sell things, how to stay in touch with customers using email – basically everything we did before the internet…we could now do online!

Now, with all these clients running successful sites, Paul, one of my colleagues challenged me to prove what I claimed on stage – that you could start a whole business from a single idea and that you can sell anything on the internet.

He said, "You can't do that." I said, "You absolutely can." He said, "What would you sell?"

We were having dinner in a Chinese restaurant at the time, and I looked around: "I could probably do a video on how to fold napkins," because there was a lot of folded napkins on the tables. That just struck me for an idea. He said, "You can't do that." I said, "I can." He said, "Do you know how to fold napkins?" I said, "I don't, but I could probably film one of the girls here that folds napkins and sell that." "You can't do that."

I got up, I went to the manager and I asked him if it would be okay to film one of his staff folding napkins: "If you let me film, I'll give you 10 copies of the DVD for your best 10 customers, to give to them on Chinese New Year." He said, "Sure!"

I went back to the table and said, "I'm filming on Thursday, and I'll have a DVD by the weekend. It'll be edited and ready to sell." He was like, "You can't do that." I said, "I'm doing it."

We filmed 18 napkin folds, edited the footage, got a voice-over, bought in Royalty Free Music and created a DVD Master. I ordered up some cases, designed and printed a sleeve and the product was ready to take to the market

Traffic and Conversion Mastery

And I knew I needed to promote and sell it using all the ways I'd shown people how to do things in my workshops actually worked.

I launched the DVD with a Press Release, which was picked up all around the world, Canada, USA, Australia, as well as UK. Lots of newspaper coverage, several TV shows and I even found myself explaining how to fold a napkin on the radio!

I always made sure to mention the domain name and retail price…! Next came YouTube, where I took the original footage and made a trailer and linked back to the site.

After optimizing for Google I moved onto eBay and that was an eye-opener. It showed that sales would peak on Valentine's Day, Mother's Day and Christmas. I learned I wasn't in the educational market; I was in the Gift Market!

Every day, my email would be peppered with orders from all over the world, and I would be burn the DVDs, print a sleeve, pack a compliment slip and even a free napkin, pack them up and take my daily walk to the Post Office to ship them out.

I could share the insights with my client's course delegates and… test… test… test…

From S3 to eZs3

Now while that was going, Bill Myers came out with a software product called MemberGate, and he invited various people to go along to a workshop to see how he was going to use it to help manage his business. I was one of two guys who flew out from the UK to see this software. I was interested in how it could automate online payments and keep client information out of the public domain. I think we've all come across variations of recurring businesses in our lives - mine goes all the way back to subscribing to Marvel Comics when I was a younger boy.

Now, Bill demonstrated the software and I really liked it. Even better, everybody that came to that workshop got a free copy in exchange for being Beta Testers. What a fantastic and generous opportunity!

Lot of the guys that took that software away went on to do very well with it.

For my part, I found myself selling the software to the UK Government, so they could build portals that were secure, provided restricted access to certain information and were very easy to set up and run.

I then became the support guy in the UK for MemberGate, so I got really quite close to the software.

Still looking for my own Membership site, and still posting out Napkin DVDs, I wanted to figure out a way to cut out the burning, packing and posting. Basically, I was looking for a way to distribute video quickly and easily... but only to those who had paid for it!

Amazon to the rescue with their Simple Storage Service... S3. This was a breakthrough in service and pricing: A 'pay-as-you-go' on-demand hosting and bandwidth deal. It meant that if you had a lot of viewers you paid, but if you didn't, you didn't pay anything. That was a brand new way to calculate your overhead and it suited me to the ground.

However, Amazon wanted to attract the geeks who were setting up the new dot coms of that era. The really big accounts, which meant their platform was extremely technical to use. You kind of had to know a lot of stuff before you went in; you had to be technically competent to use it.

On top of that, they also then bolted on a support system that was expensive with an up-front payment required. So they really kind of alienated a lot of people.

Traffic and Conversion Mastery

Luckily for me, I was employing Steve Hicks by this time, an Oxford University Master of Science in Computing, and he solved all the riddles that Amazon posed and set-up a Software-As-A Service for hosting video, all wrapped up in MemberGate and called it eZs3.

That meant you didn't have to understand what Amazon was doing, and all the rules, you just went to Amazon, signed up, and came back to eZs3, and it would just work. You uploaded your video. You create a player. You got the embed code. You put it on your webpage. And you are done It was very popular. People really liked it. At its high point we were over 5,000 members paying $20 per month. We added an affiliate program, so that members could reduce the cost of their membership by getting other people to join. We introduced improved marketing features, so that videos can show an order form or PayPal button or a survey, during the playback or at the end.

All we wanted to do then, and all we keep doing now: make it easy to use.

And while we focus on that, MemberGate runs the business for us!

When I think of all the businesses I have advised, trained and coached, subscription is my favourite business model.

When I think of the transition from print to digital. From bricks to clicks. From local to global.

No matter what the business, to grow it you have to get the basics right:

1. Increase the number of Transactions – more customers, extend range
2. Increase the Value of the Transaction – link sales, add on sales, price rise
3. Increase the Frequency of Transactions – annual to half-yearly, monthly to weekly, weekly to daily

4. Increase the Lifetime of the relationship – loyalty schemes
5. Decrease the cost of Customer Acquisition – measure and test
6. Provide a great product and service – exceed expectations

MemberGate allows us to deliver on all these fronts and provides essential reports and data, making our lives easier.

There are some great advantages of a subscription business, and certainly one of them has to be the fact that it's much more attractive to a buy-out offer because of the known regular income, and actually it's well known that the angels and the VCs will pay extra for a business with subscription or continuity. Several times the multiple of the turnover because of its quantifiable and reliable income.

Now, I've been providing support to clients of MemberGate over the years, and I've proven that it's a sustainable and profitable business.

I think that 'need to prove' has never gone away and recently I invested in a security business and added a subscription to their product and service package. This has strengthened the business and allowed us to leverage the resources of MemberGate.

Just moving the original site onto MemberGate improved the SEO and increased traffic. It also meant prospects could order right off page. We provide clients with support using the HelpDesk and we have articles, tutorials and videos that only members can access.

On top of that, there's the in-built Affiliate Program, which we have tweaked to allow us to attract, build and manage our world-wide dealerships.

Membergate isn't just a web-site builder... it's a business builder!

Once again, I am proving that you can digitize a traditional business using the right tools, and marketing savvy.

Looking to the Future

Many online businesses are going to take a hit with the blow-back from the Ashley Madison hack that happened last year. That's caused some real upset with the credit card distributors - your Visas, MasterCards and Amexes. They are not happy about how easy it has been for masses of customer data to be stolen, and anybody in business on the internet will have to prove that they've got a very secure system.

Take this as a heads up: check that your sites and systems meet the standards set by the credit card industry - PCIDSS. If not, they'll start by fining you, and then they'll move on to taking away your privilege of being able to take credit cards.

The biggest example of that so far has been the struggle that Click Bank has had getting into compliance.

Click Bank's a big business, and they can afford the experts and resources need to comply, but the challenge with open source software is going to be open source hacks. And another challenge with open source software, like WordPress, is plugin management. When somebody updates a plugin to make this work or that work, whether it's a shopping cart or a subscription plugin or a fancy image editor or moving widget, all of those have the opportunity to be hacked. Wordpress posted an official update last October, and it just stopped all the sites working.

For myself, I am taking over at MemberGate!

I want MemberGate to be more accessible to more people. I particularly would like it to be more accessible to traditional businesses, a solid and reliable option for businesses that are stable.

I've been running eZs3, and it's been working for 10 years, and sometimes people are very short sighted when they launch their website, often changing it every two years.

I want them to be thinking about a much more solid web-business and much more stable platform and one that they can grow with and build their business with.

So that's what I'm looking to do with MemberGate. I'm looking to make it a fundamentally sound proposition to run a business on the internet, and within that there is already bundled subscription, payment, cart, affiliate program, video, image management, SEO, and all the other features and bells and whistles that are included.

You won't have to get plugins from other sites and install and manage them, you won't get the downtime and distractions, because they are already built into MemberGate.

We're just going to make it a more robust business, a more robust service, and we hope to bring people in, because it's quite easy to migrate to MemberGate. All you need to do is get us access to your current information and Graphics package, we'll help you set the graphics up, and you can be adding content the next day!

If you don't have a subscription revenue stream in your business, head over to MemberGate.com, and let's see if we can help

About Tom Cone

Tom has been a Marketing specialist for 20 years, and was appointed by Rural Development Commission and Yorkshire Forward to help businesses in Yorkshire.

He is also the Marketing Director at BoatWarden, which manufactures and distributes security and protection systems for luxury powerboats, speedboats and yachts.

Tom recently launched OutboardWarden.com at the London Boat Show, Jan 2016.

He is the founder of Software As A Service (eZs3.com) - which has powered 4.2 Billion videos.

Tom's specialties include: Sales, direct marketing, internet marketing, video marketing, PR, exhibitions, product development and coaching.

To connect with Tom, visit him at MemberGate.com.

Profit in business comes from repeat customers, customers that boast about your project or service, and that bring friends with them.

~W. Edwards Deming~

Chapter 4

Quit Doing It Wrong!

By Jason Myers

Do you own a business? Quit doing it wrong! In the wise words of Bob Newhart – Stop IT!!

You *can* do it right, but you first have to realize what not to do. Now that I have your attention, read on.

Let's examine what most business owners do to make a living.

Look at John, a business owner in the information marketing business. He's a success, or so it seems. He has a hit product in a hot niche and has had progressively bigger launches using affiliates. He's only had a small batch of "failures" and he counts himself in the winners' circle amongst people on the annual marketer's cruise. Let's say he is in the top 5% of the 400 cruisers in terms of income.

Is John a success? No.

Here's why he is just doing it plain wrong. He has one business, one source of income via his info products. He tells me he is diversified. He has an ascension model taught by guru after guru. Low-end to high-end products and an eco-system of cross-sell and upsell. To learn more, I launch into an exploratory conversation wherein I dispel the myth that he is either stable, successful or diversified.

He has a business. It's one business. A single point of failure in my experience. He has a niche, it relies upon a successful funnel using LinkedIn and Facebook Marketing. He uses low-end, trip-wire style entry points and moves people to more profitable products. Regardless of his product offering, he is only one policy change from have an advertising account shut down. He is only one fumble from losing his inbound marketing traffic.

He goes on to tell me that I don't understand his business and that he also has a robust posse of affiliate marketing partners that insulate him from traffic issues. I agree that they are a productive source of traffic. We discuss that affiliates can be great and that the ideal scenario is actually an offer that converts from cold traffic. We then agree that his business cannot thrive on affiliate traffic alone.

I go on to share a story of a stubborn, mule-headed friend of mine that saw his business spiral from $60,000 a month to less than $6,000 per month over a span of only 24-hours. In other words, he wasn't in control. And neither are you – Facebook, LinkedIn or Affiliates are in control.

If you have enjoyed $60,000 per month in cash flow and now you have to fight, scrape and hustle to get $6,000, the entire world may seem to have turned against you. If only he would have listened to me...

At this point you might be getting as depressed as he was. Do not despair, there is a solution. There is a way to protect yourself from this meltdown: Diversification.

Do you view your business as an investment or a cash machine?

For me, the right viewpoint is as an investment. That's right, it is an investment. Since it is an investment, it should be a part of your overall investment portfolio. It should NOT be the only thing you are invested in. It also should not be the only business you are invested in.

Most business coaches, mentors and gurus will tell you to find something you're passionate about and throw yourself into the deep in... go all-in. They will also tell you that focus is needed to get it going and to be successful. Maybe their right, in the beginning. My view is different.

Think about this: when your business is getting going you are running on adrenaline. Nothing can stop you. Then it throws off cash and fuels your lifestyle and at some invisible, usually imperceptible point you become accustomed to the lifestyle it affords you. Maybe your personal life changes and changing family needs soon dictate that you take less and less risks. That shift in risk-tolerance is the riskiest behavior of them all. Your very livelihood is now, unknowingly, built upon a fragile house of cards.

Now all of your eggs are in one business "basket." One macro change in the economy, change in platform rules, traffic methods, system outage or random issue and you're dead in the water. It doesn't have to be that way.

The solution is to employ what I call geometric entrepreneurialism. This G.E. method consists of a framework, as follows:

1. Strategize - Understand that you should not be the long-term primary operator of the business
2. Execute – tactically, the things that matter
3. Systematize – standardize and document
4. Delegate – get out of the day to day
5. Inspect – adjust based on a solid, systematized feedback loop
6. Lead - the business through changes
7. Add-on - new businesses

Then the geometric success comes from - Rinse and Repeat!

Step 3 is one that very few owners accomplish to the degree they need to. If they do make it past step 3, they fall way short of Step 7 of the GE framework. It is the most important piece and one most business owners fail to accomplish. This "Add-on" step of the framework is about creating a new, diversified business as soon as the prior business is delegated and tweaked to operate "mostly" without you.

The power of this concept, this GE framework, is that you build a portfolio of independent businesses that operate separately in different spaces/niches and that can be sold independently. A key to this is that they must each be in different parts of their lifecycle, each needing something different from you. As you sell them, they each unlock a step-function jump in your cash in the bank. This creates the ultimate goal – which is: Geometric Wealth.

A common rebuttal of this practice is that it is hard enough to run one business. If you say this, you're right. If you say that the business will be bigger if you focus 110% on one business and to this you might be right. You might also be wrong, especially if that one business encounters rough waters.

You might also say, look at all the wealthy people who started a business and sold it for a gazillion dollars. Yes, but look more closely – lightning can strike, but they have since employed a more investor mindset than an owner mindset. They evolved. Look at poster children for this: Elon Musk, Richard Branson and Warren Buffet. They have stakes in several businesses and are not looking for lightning to strike. They don't need it. They can hit a bunch of singles from a variety of endeavors and create wealth faster than waiting, banking on a homerun to hit "one day, someday, maybe."

Diving more deeply into the concept, let's look at this image depicting multiple businesses launched sequentially and requiring different oversight:

Multiply Yourself:

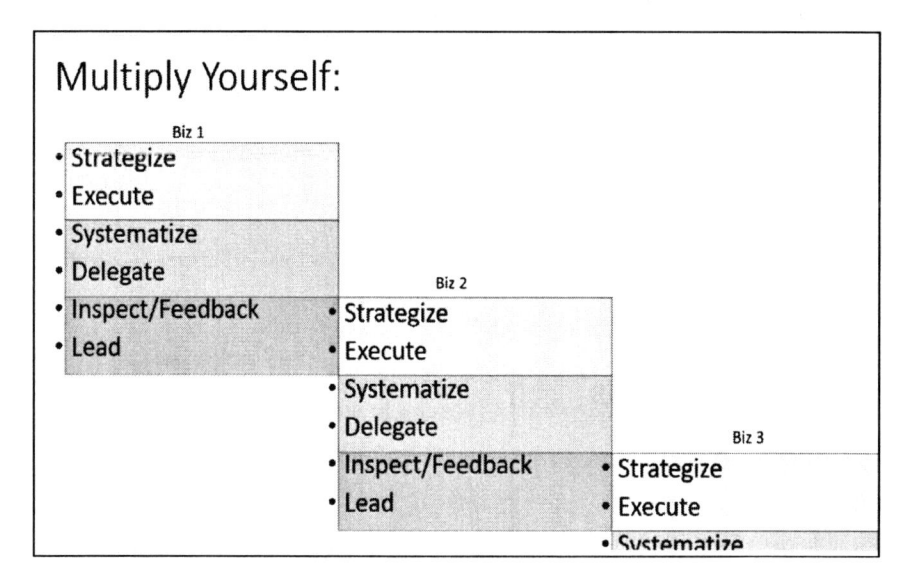

Biz 1
- Strategize
- Execute
- Systematize
- Delegate
- Inspect/Feedback
- Lead

Biz 2
- Strategize
- Execute
- Systematize
- Delegate
- Inspect/Feedback
- Lead

Biz 3
- Strategize
- Execute
- Systematize

The power of this is that it allows you to assume the role of Chairman/Chairwoman of this portfolio of diversified investments of both your time and your money. This is a more powerful, more profitable and wealthier view of being an entrepreneur than that held by 99.5% of business owners.

Chairman - that sounds great, but don't you think you have the bandwidth to run a whole group of companies? On the contrary, the model gets very powerful as you realize that the highest and best use of your time is as the visionary leader that creates, delegates and repeats.

You see, the DNA of most entrepreneurs is filled with a few common components that this model harnesses:

1. There is always another idea
2. There is not enough time to execute all of them
3. It's easy to get bored with even a very successful business

In the GE model, you have the idea, get it going, find someone to run it, provide oversight and leadership – meanwhile you use cash flow from it to fund a new business while you simply rinse and repeat as many times as you dare. Think about this: how big would Berkshire Hathaway be if

Warren Buffet were driving a train on Burlington Northern every day? Would SpaceX AND Tesla and Solar City exist if Elon decided to start and operate one business, one idea at a time? The light bulbs should be going off by now – you get it now.

Finally, there is an entrepreneurial model congruent with your core DNA!

If you feel that this is easier said than done, you're right. If you think that you don't even know what you don't know about this GE model, you'd be right. I have spent a career doing this and have built a global organization of people accomplishing this. I also have limited slots for my upcoming:

2016 Geometric Entrepreneurialism Mastermind - GEM

I'm offering cruisers a special mastermind to work with me and fellow cruisers for the next 12 months, concluding with our group sharing celebration during next year's cruise at a private party I am hosting in the Steakhouse, with fine wine, food and new friendships to last a lifetime.

Make no mistake, this isn't for everyone and may not be for you. It also isn't cheap. For this level of access to me and my methods, I have recently charged people up to $150,000. It is available to a very limited number of cruisers on this 10th anniversary cruise for a special, "we all love Captain Lou" one-time investment in yourself of only $5,000.

Here is what to expect in the next 12 months:

<u>Join while on the cruise and attend my private **GEM**astermind faststart kickoff in my Grand Suite</u>.

Then we'll have a 2-day group event in March in Palm Beach, FL where we deep dive on you, your business and build the GEroadmap for you. We'll have weekly group calls for one year. We'll have two separate 3-

day mastermind gatherings at great venues. You'll get access to a private online group accessible only to **GEM**astermind members wherein you can keep the momentum, accountability and success going --- all year long.

As a cruise bonus: I'll even give you two private 30-minute coaching calls with me to use whenever you or your business needs it throughout the year.

Listen, if you keep doing business the way you've been doing it, you'll keep getting the results you've been getting. Now is the time to take the right step into the **GEM**astermind to build your entrepreneurial investment portfolio and finally get the return on investment you deserve. Join now – find me at Pizza and Profits.

About Jason Myers

Jason Myers is a pilot, inventor, serial entrepreneur, author, and perpetual sponge for knowledge. He has started, invested in and sold many successful offline and online companies since 1991. He is often referred to as a business ninja with a swiss army knife, able to diagnose and fix nearly any issue. Growing businesses with effective marketing and operations is a passion of his.

Jason is Co-founder of CXO Collective International, a Private Equity firm with a non-profit Global Entreprenurial organization that harnesses the triad of: Capital, Talent and Opportunities. CXO focuses on acquiring stakes in companies and growing them for fun and profit. CXO Collective has grown to attract members in 30 U.S. states and 8 countries. Members can earn performance based stock/equity/cash incentives compensation in the form of consulting fees and stock. To learn more, or to join the movement, head on over to http://www.cxocollective.com/cruise

You can also contact Jason directly on Linkedin https://www.linkedin.com/in/myjason or via email at: jason.myers@cxocollective.com

Chapter 5

Vetting For Yourself and Your Business

By Mike Hill

I guess you could say that I 'm one of those "success stories" you see on TV... Only thing is, I'm the one watching TV and I still can't believe it.

Not so long ago, after having been fired from a call center that I was managing, (for partying too much) I was unemployed, living in a barn, still smoking weed, and trying to figure out what I wanted to do when I grew up.

In one of those crazy coincidences that life can bring, I answered an ad for a receptionist working for an Internet company. "I'll start for $6 an hour", I said. "Just give me a chance to prove myself and within a year I will be running your company."

Well, within a year a couple of my ideas took off, and I was the Vice President. By the end of the second year I had outgrown the company and went out on my own as a traffic & conversion consultant.

I was hired by a few companies for conversion optimization, with the option to be a "super affiliate" for them. Thankfully, the time I spent working for my last employer had really served me well. The business model worked very well for over a decade, and I believe would still work well today for anyone with my type of experience and offering.

I get asked frequently how I "got to where I am today"... the answer is simple - frustration and drive! Frustration with the fact that marketers believed they had to manipulate customers, and the drive to change that belief.

I have always held the contention that you don't need to manipulate people into buying your products. You simply need to be truthful and clear. Instead of taking control, give them full and unlimited control. Being open and honest, and most importantly, yourself, will result in the right people connecting with you and your product. My being at this point in my career and life today is a direct result of my frustration, and my inner drive to change a struggling industry.

The important part to remember is that the world continues to get smaller and smaller. Your brand must stay consistent to its cause now more than ever. What you say today matters, and what you believe matters most.

It Wasn't Always Easy

I've had to face many problems as I grew my business. One of the largest issues I would face with clients was overcoming their past programming.

Let me explain.

There are two sets of problems you will tend to encounter when working with both clients and customers; first, there's the psychological problems (which are always the bigger obstacles), then second, there are the tangible or physical issues (these are usually what they report to you as the thing you are to fix).

The psychological issues for many clients I've helped over the years mostly stem from the fact they simply didn't believe high levels of sales could be made without some sort of manipulation and removal of control.

From the process side of things, clients tend to want to keep sending traffic to a website that is simply not created with cold traffic in mind. Many had been programmed to believe that if they simply made a "squeeze page" and sent traffic that they would be wealthy beyond their wildest dreams.

And for some, this came true when they started sending traffic from what is called "warm traffic" or "JV." This only re-affirmed what they had been told. Unfortunately, this is what we call a "false positive" in the industry.

YES! When you send potential customers with a warm referral, you can get away with an awful lot of bad business practices. However, once there is not someone credible to speak on your behalf, you have to now start to use real and timeless marketing traditions. (In fairness, many of those 1980's traditions are also not working now, but that's another story.)

In today's world, putting a little effort into deeper communication, multi path sequencing, true consumer psychology, buying behaviors, and heck, just a decent auto responder sequence that builds trust is now a foundation, and not a window dressing. Each of these additions and more result in higher and higher conversions, more shares, and exponentially higher returns in paid traffic.

Essentially, many think the solution to the problem is to simply shove traffic at dwindling sales, when the real solution is to shove TIME at the problem, THEN shove big volumes of traffic after the time had been invested to build the best courtship possible.

We have to develop our own systems, which is based 100% on the psychology of the client themselves! Not their business, not their sales cycle, but a solution that frees the business owner from the business, while also increasing sales and brand alignment. After 15 years of consulting, we have seen countless clients who THINK they want more sales, but when it came time to review the psychology behind the business, they really wanted an entirely different model that truly resonated with them as a human. Once that is in place, then the business explodes (providing they can believe).

A perfect example is a client who was running infomercials. I looked at his business, I looked at him as an individual and I looked at his true outcome.

Then I asked, "What do you really want from this?"

He told me his private dream and vision, which was NOTHING like what he was doing. So it was easy to say, "Great. Let's reverse engineer the outcome and build for that exact thing! You want to be able to help tens of thousands of people. You want them to know you are trustworthy. You don't want to advertise the real you. Fantastic! You're starting an entirely new company, and we're going to change the company name, the company principles, company psychology, and all advertising."

He agreed to do exactly as was outlined, and now eclipses every other player in his market place, and is moving his life right into the next branch of the dream he had always had.

The hardest part of it all is when others think "I can just copy that guy"... after all, that's what we are taught, right?

Well, you can't copy someone else's truth.

What we do is get to the root of our client's truth, remove the BS programming, limiting beliefs, (I've seen 100 million dollar CEO's with limiting beliefs, so don't think that you are the only one), and we help the client to share an unfiltered version of themselves with their customers and the world. The end result is an amazingly resonate message that not everyone will align with, but it will definitely attract the right people who your company can help.

I make sure that their starting and ending messages resonate with their outcome because if it doesn't, remember, the client will always sabotage whatever they're working on, because, at some level, they don't really want it to succeed. They may say verbally they want it to succeed, but in actuality, the fear of "what if I change it and it all breaks" is very real. Fear kills sales. We don't have client failures, but when we did, they were always the result of someone not willing to take ownership in a process. You can't outsource ownership. You can't outsource caring, and you can't outsource your own energy.

2016 is the year our company helps itself. And if they are pure of heart and pure of intent, we will probably help a handful of people who are ready to take ownership, and are ready to help us change the world just as we have with a small industry.

Any potential client for 2016 will definitely have to go through a tough psychological background check. They will have to be fearless and willing to accept the results of self-discovery. They must be willing to face their own demons and slay them right in front of someone else. They will have to have the right reasons for being in business. The vetting process for 2016 is intense, but it's necessary.

What we do is not cookie cutter. Because we are not cookies! You are not a cookie! Your brand is not a cookie. You and your brand are a living and breathing entity. We have the obligation to be sure that we are empowering those who have the right cause and intent for humanity.

Paid advertising is POWER. And that power must be used responsibly.

The power is limitless, and I have seen it used to hurt mothers, grandmothers, families, and children. They are not "unique visitors", they are friends and families.

Our typical client is someone who has felt the need and the desire to change the world at very large levels (the kind of person who was cast out from social circles for being unrealistic). We crave working with others who dream at a global level. Someone who understands the value of putting together a positive and competent supporting team. Someone who understands that just because you've tested it twice doesn't mean it didn't work. It simply means that you found two ways not to test again under those exact same conditions. Our ideal client has a budget that says, "I've got the business balls to be able to get this job done. I'm not going to shy away." They are not going to look at a 10K spend and ask us to "prove ourselves." The ONLY constant is traffic. The variable here is YOU. What are you able to do, what are you willing to do, and what is your reason for staying the course?

We get asked all the time to "spend a million dollars per month." That seems to be the magic carrot that small time players think will get them attention. I always ask, "OK, and what are you willing to pay the team that spends that money for you in month 1, month 2, month 3?" I'm shocked at the times that the answer is "2K, 3k, or even 5K." These people are asking to get the best support possible, but only want to pay out two tenths of one percent to get that job done? That's lunacy.

The stamina and understanding of core business drivers and teams is critical to any business. Do you have the proper team in place? A properly constructed and supportive team that has been collected through scientific means is far more interesting than "I've got a great team."

We quickly find teams that are sub-par, who have snowed a CEO. In fact, I did a consultation for a very well-known person in the fitness industry four or five years ago. When I arrived, I did my normal job of making everyone feel safe and comfortable. But I quickly learned some very disturbing things about the team leader. I informed the CEO, "This guy's going to quit in less than 6 months." ... He replied "No way! He's been with me forever and had huge plans."... I replied, "No really... He's going to quit, and you're paying me to train him! This is a waste for you... You need to be in this room."

I'm sure you know the outcome. He quit, and the CEO was elated that he had been in the room at my request during training. The team lie is one of the biggest we tell ourselves as company owners. Heck, if we didn't put together a good team, then we would have to admit failure, and we can't have that... Or can we?

Putting the wrong peg in the wrong hole happens to us all, myself included! Hiring because we like someone is the kiss of death. Hiring your team, and ensuring they are driven by your common goal will help my job and yours go a LOT smoother.

In fact, I prefer working with a client who's fallen down a few times on his or her own! This usually leads to a diminished ego and clears the way for willingness to accept new ideas and drastic change.

Does Size Matter to Success?

Let's look at the size of an organization. Usually we see companies with 5-10 individuals who run the ship as a good size (not counting support staff, outsources, etc.). Any more than that and it gets too political.

If you hire a competent consultant, someone will want them gone. Because no matter how much you as the CEO think or hope that your entire team is for the best interest of the company, someone is not in agreement. And in many cases, it can be many people who are waiting for the other shoe to drop.

I tell all our clients, "Someone's going to ask you to fire me and tell you you're wasting your money." This is usually the person who is either A: undervalued by the company, or B: overvalued by the company. In every case, I will identify which of the two and tell the CEO accordingly. "You have a star with Person A, listen to them finally and you will do well."

As for spend and revenue, our clients traditionally earn well over a million per year. Most are over the five million mark. But if the team is right and the product is right, current sales volume is not really a factor. Remember, we had our sample client above re-build his entire business. So he literally had no sales at all. But he did have a back-end process, very little ego, a high level of business stamina, and a drive! For media buying we recommend a minimum 50-100K budget to quick start your endeavor. Our minimum engagement fee for paid traffic is $10,000 per month. We actually had a client who only had a 20K budget, who paid us our 10K monthly minimum for 6 months just to have us set up some structure. He was a venture capitalist, so he saw the long term value.

How long should you test and what is a good time to look for a return? Good question, but an elusive and tricky one. Your success in buying traffic is determined by the conversion ratio of the process itself and not by the traffic.

Traffic sources change a little over time but not by much. They'll change from publisher to publisher and as technology changes. There will be new breakthroughs in technologies and in targeting capabilities, but the traffic itself really doesn't change much. For us it's not a factor of how much time it would take to be successful. It's how *quickly* can the client execute on the suggestions of each phase of testing. I would not like to see any test run less than 90 days. 90 days would give you enough opportunity, but I have had companies take and stretch a 90 day test into a two year test, and sadly paying minimums the entire time, because they were not willing to let go of bad staffing, hire new staffing, dedicate their own time, or believe the lie that they've "got a great team."

Luckily for us, we're very sought after, so we can afford to be very picky. Because of the client vetting process and individual vetting process, we've had clients with us for years. If we do lose a client, it was either planned from the start, or foretold by us. Someone will come to us asking for a "kick start" and we know they want to move traffic teams internally. We know we're not keeping this client forever from the beginning and it's agreed.

Many companies are now seeing the value of bringing a team in-house, but they need a good priming to get that happening. I recognize that in these clients who are trying to hide that fact, so I just come out and say, "Let's get you started. Let's get you ramped up, and I know you're going to end up bringing this in-house, because I'm not an idiot. After 16 years of this, I can read between your words, so let's just get you started." So we create a structure that makes this intent work. In a year or so they are usually good to go.

Again, it's all about the vetting for yourself and for your business. I personally only want clients that are going to be successful.

Here's a good example: A friend referred a client, and in our vetting process a few things in our conversation made me realize "this isn't going to work." She was basically blaming her team for all inefficiencies and problems in her company. She blamed everyone else but herself, and EVERY single statement I made, there was some excuse or reason why it was the way it was.

She had already paid $25,000 to come for a 1 day consultation in my home office, but I made the decision to send her money back. "I'm sending you back your money. I'm sorry, but you're not going to be a good client for me." Oh boy did she freak out. She eventually found a way to get me to say yes, but I warned her that I didn't think it was going to be helpful for her for the EXACT reasons I'm telling you. At the end of a six month engagement, we were still only a few weeks into the project. She was brilliant! Not a bad person, just not ready for our way of doing things.

There Are No Guarantees in life.

"Can you guarantee this is going to work?"...

When I get this question, I always do the exact thing I'm told to never do. Laugh in the client's face. I'm not meaning to be mean, it's just so incredibly ridiculous to think that I could ever guarantee that someone else will do what they are supposed to do. If you are ever asked that, or if you ever find yourself asking that question of someone else, stop for a moment and ask yourself "why am I asking this?"

We have found that this question is either A: an automatic response based on social conditioning, or B: an attempt to prevent one's self from fully investing into the option (like a safety bridge for mental health).

Of course after chuckling a bit, I always say, "Not only no, but hell no, and I am not 100% sure you're the right type of client for us." And I explain the above paragraph and ask, "Which are you"?

In 16 years I had ONE person ask for a refund, and that was back in 2001 when I used to fly to their office. My lesson was simple after him. Never go into someone else's office where they are the king of the jungle and subjected to distraction and a lack of focus. Even though I wrote a script which dramatically altered the call center conversion rate, the client was wrong from the start, and I knew it. Trust your instincts!

What Makes a Real Success?

The first question our top clients ask is, "Who do I need to hire, and how can you help me make sure that I have the right team in place to execute all of the things that need to be done?"

The second question should be "Are my assets the right assets?"

Asset collection is critical to a solid plan. So many spend such a small amount of time collecting assets. You should be asking yourself, "do I have enough assets, and do I have the right team to be able to perform all of the functions and roles that are going to be necessary for mass traffic?" Remember, it is a continual editing process.

The final question should be "what am I willing to give up to make this happen?" Because guess what, you will have to give up something, and if you are not, it will never work.

A solid ad campaign should have dozens of landing pages within a couple years and tons of variations. Some deep psychology on every single theme set of keywords that are driving people to the website and so much more. There should be multiple avatar profiles broken down so that they know exactly who they're talking to. Drive for that 10-20% conversion rate. To get to that point, you need assets, you need a plan, and you must, above all else, be willing to get naked to your own future.

About Mike Hill

Mike Hill is most recently known for his work as founder of the incredibly successful and influential group "Internet Marketing Supers", with over 14,000 members and a list of over 9,000 waiting to get in. His experience over 16 years as a marketing coach, media buyer, conversion specialist and empathic marketer have allowed him to cultivate his unique ability to guide and influence business owners in finding a more fulfilling and rewarding business life. Mike's experiences in creating and managing campaigns that touch billions has made him consciously aware of the profound power that advertisers have, and how to use that power responsibly. His only marketing training product, CPA Tsunami, released in 2008 broke new ground in content delivery expectations for high price point products, and set the bar for over-delivery. Every time Mike takes the stage, his consistent message of doing what is right, over what "appears to be" most profitable, wins crowds and hearts. With the change from profit to passion, Mike is one of the most influential voices of 2016 you have likely heard as echo's in other brands. Learn more about Mike at **http://mikehill.me**

Chapter 6

Mentorship, Masterminding and Coaching

How We Redesigned Our Mastermind & Coaching Program To Help Our Clients Create Better, Faster Results

By Daven Michaels

I'm Daven Michaels, founder and CEO of 123Employee, the premier outsourcing centers in the Philippines. We have hundreds of employees. We work with entrepreneurs all over the globe, some of the biggest thought leaders on the planet. We do internet marketing, social media, telemarketing, all the busy stuff in the business, so they can focus on the income generating activities in the business and the things that really juice them and excite them. Our mission at 123Employee is to rescue lifestyle-starved entrepreneurs, give them their time back and their lives back, and we love doing it.

It's really in my DNA. I've been an entrepreneur for well over three decades. Our VP, Beejal Parmer, has been an entrepreneur for over 15 years as well. It's what we do. It's what we love, and at the same time we are in what I would like to think of as the second phase in our business. We're certainly not turning our backs on entrepreneurs who've really been our bread and butter for so many years, but we have big initiatives in place to go after larger clients. We are starting to attract those C level clients, and we like doing that as well.

I didn't start off in this business. It's sort of an entrepreneur story. I started my business when I was 15. I don't know what kind of idiot would start their business at 15, but I did. That's because I was an only child, and I literally had nobody around to tell me that I couldn't do it. I thought I could do anything. That was awesome and challenging. I fell on my butt several times before I figured it out. I was very fortunate. I graduated high school a couple years early. Not because I was smarter than anybody else, but just because I hated it. I doubled up on my work, and I was out of high school by 16.

By the time I was 17 I was going to college, and I was very fortunate. Today there's like a million entrepreneurship programs, but back then there were zero. There were no entrepreneurship degrees. When I was going to Junior College I met these two gentlemen, and they were prolific entrepreneurs. They were entrepreneurs back when there weren't a lot of entrepreneurs, back in the 50s and the 60s. They made millions and millions of dollars doing all types of things. They were the first guys to ever put an offer on a box of cereal. They made millions just from that alone, back in the day when millions was like crazy money.

They were retired and bored, and so they decided to be professors at the local Junior College. They taught a one-year entrepreneurship program. It was like a one-year immersion. I took the class and being the youngest kid, they took me under their wing. They taught me a lot, but what they really taught me is that putting these crazy ideas to fruition was possible, and that I could do it. I begged, borrowed, and stole everything I could to start my very first business; it was a clothing company on Melrose. I started that as a kid not even old enough to enter into a legal lease.

The odds of my success were nil, but a funny thing happened. Literally days after we opened MTV came on the air, changed the face of music, and changed our lives. We were working with these bands that had nothing going on. Most were playing in their garage, and within about 90 days most of those bands had record deals. Within about a year they were selling millions of albums. We rode that wave. It was a wild time. We ended up designing clothing for some of the biggest bands of the 80s and 90s. That really began my career and showed me that I could actually do it.

From there I went on to do a lot of different businesses. I was in the telecommunications business. Then I ended up in internet. Then I fell into the outsourcing business. It was a division of our company. I was actually in Asia quite a bit because of my music publishing deal, and so we started a small company over there to serve our clients. Unfortunately it was a very bumpy road. The infrastructure wasn't there back then, but we muddled through it. Today we have a very successful company. It's exciting, and we love doing it. Every day is a new challenge and opportunity.

Expansion is the Key

This chapter isn't really so much about the outsourcing business.

It's really about the 3 things that I attribute all of my success to: Mentorship, Masterminding and Coaching. I'm a huge product of the product. I believe in Mentorship, Mastermind and Coaching, and I utilize it on so many different levels. If we're talking about Masterminding, I'm in many Masterminds. We've been doing Masterminds for our clients for many years. I'll talk more about that in a minute. My best ideas, my best alliances, my best partners have come from Masterminds. The most success and the most accelerated success I've had, both in life and in business, have come from Coaching.

Finally, Mentorship, because people who follow my career have seen me have a lot of success in a lot of different businesses, from the fashion business to the entertainment business to the outsourcing business to investments in music and television, and now working on a full feature film. They ask, "What is your secret to success?" I've explained that it was really a formula that I created in the early days, in my early 20s, for business. It came from one of my earliest mentors, and his name was Hal. It went back to when I was in the music business. When I was in the music business there's a formulaic approach to pop songs. It was basically verse, chorus, verse, chorus, bridge, and chorus. Back then I used to think to myself, "Could there be a formulaic approach to business?" I really didn't know. It was really just an idea and a thought at the time.

It went back to when I sold my second company, which was my telecommunications company. I was in the paging business. If you're reading this right now my guess is that at one time you may have had a pager, but I guarantee you don't have one today. That's because pagers are a perfect example of a business that technology swallowed. There is no paging business today, because today there's a cell phone business. That's one of the biggest businesses in the world. Back then pagers were the cell phones of the era, if you will. We were in the paging business, and I had a great business. I was making a lot of money, and it was one of my first businesses. It was a huge win, but I can't really take a lot of responsibility for it. I was just in the right place at the right time. I guess I can take a little more responsibility than that, but really it just took off and it was really exciting.

I was a young kid walking around with wads of cash in my pockets, nice cars, nice threads, and great food. It was just a blast. I was probably making more money than a kid should. I knew that my days were numbered, because we knew that cell phones were coming out in a couple years, and everything was going to change. The consensus in the industry was that cell phones would come out, and more pagers would get sold. That initially actually did make sense, because back then it was $0.50 a minute for cell phone service. Today I'd compare that to maybe a dollar or two a minute. What most people would do is they would page their friend, and then their friend would call them back, but I knew that that wouldn't last forever. I knew that the bottom would fall out of the cell phone business, and eventually minutes would become very inexpensive, and there would be no pagers.

At the time paging businesses were huge. They were the cell phones of their time. There were these huge multinational companies that were traded at 20, 40, 60 times multiples that sold pagers. That's what they did. One of these big companies, one of our suppliers, offered to buy me out. I remember they flew me out to Santa Barbara. They wined me and dined me and made me a very generous cash offer, but it wasn't enough money to have me leave the business. It was really a year's revenue or a couple years' revenue. I just felt like the business was worth more. So I turned down that offer. I wasn't sure that was the best move, but I knew that the writing was on the wall. I had about two years or less, 24 months, to sell my business. I knew that every month the value of my business would probably keep going down.

I reached out to a gentleman by the name of Hiram, who was the biggest business broker in our vertical, and I said, "Hiram, I want to sell my company. Find me a suitor." He said, "I'll take care of it." He whittled it down to two. There were only really two perfect suitors. One was a guy, Robert. Robert was a crook. There was no way I could do a deal with Robert. There was no way I could guarantee I'd get paid. The other was a guy by the name of Hal. He was a business maverick. We all wanted to be like Hal when we grew up. He was probably in his late 60s. He looked and acted like Telly Savalas. He was the coolest cat you ever met. He always wore the coolest threads, and he always had a beautiful woman on his arm. I think he'd been married about four or five times.

Hal was amazing in business. He would purchase distressed companies, clean them up, take them public, and cash out. He did it time and time again. I saw him do almost 10 of those. He was incredible. Hal owned a public company in the paging business, and there were all these big multinational public companies. Hal was a small public company. If you compare it to other private companies it was a really big company, but if you compare it to public companies it was pretty small. Hal was literally one of the last couple of public companies that hadn't been merged into any other company yet.

We just felt he was the perfect suitor for my business. Hiram worked on him for about a year, and nothing happened. One day Hal calls me out of the blue, and he says, "Daven, do you want to do this deal or what?" I said to him, "Yeah, I do." He said, "Great. Meet me at the Winchell's donut shop around the corner from my office tomorrow at noon." I said, "Okay." Hal loved donuts, so we met at Winchell's. In 45 minutes we hammered out the sale of my business, which took me five years to build. We were in 60 cities across the US. We mapped out the whole thing on a Winchell's napkin, and the deal was done.

I remember as we started hammering out the deal Hal said, "How much do you want?" I told him what I wanted. He said, "I can't do that." I said, "Actually, I think you can." I said, "I'm going to make it easy for you. I'm firm on my offer, but I'll take a note. I'll take some cash, and I'll take stock in your company." He said, "I could do that." That's because for him it was more of a paper deal. He could buy now, and pay later. So he said, "Done. I'll do that deal."

The question is, why did I do the deal? For a couple reasons. One is I thought that it was very odd that after a year all of a sudden Hal wanted to do the deal. I thought that was very bizarre. Also, I knew that Hal was the smallest company on the block, and he was the last man standing. He was the last guy that hadn't been swallowed up yet. I felt like he was a good candidate. So we did the deal. We shook hands. The deal was done, and I left for the French Riviera. I was gone for three weeks and had the time of my life. While I was gone everything was put together. My employees found out about a week before I was to come back that I had sold the company. That was a little rough, but they all had raises at the new company, so everybody was happy, and the deal was done. When I came back my company was sold.

I remember I came back, and I met Hal at his office to pick up my first check. We did cash, we did stock, and we did a note. I thought Hal is going to be my new best friend. We're in business together. We're in bed together now and we're going to be hanging out. Hal also owned 42 classic cars, so as a parting gift he gave me a 1958 pink Cadillac and a 1965 Mustang convertible with pony interior. He's a very cool guy.

Hal also had a new wife. She was gorgeous, and Hal was tickled because she was even wealthier than Hal. They were really happy. We walked outside and I'll never forget, Hal gets into his 1965 bright red El Dorado Cadillac convertible with the top down and white interior. His girl slides in, because there were no bucket seats in those cars, and nuzzled in with him. I remember watching them drive off with the top down into the sunset, literally. I remember thinking to myself, that guy is so fricking cool.

About a year or so goes by and half of his company gets bought out. My stock triples, and that moment in time changed my entire life, and really took me on to the next level. Unfortunately during that time Hal's wife had some stomach pain, and 90 days later she was dead from pancreatic cancer. Hal was devastated. He was heartbroken. At the same time I had broken up with my girl, and all of a sudden these two bachelors find themselves together in the summer in Newport Beach in California.

Hal had lost his wife. I had divorced my wife, so we were both grieving. We didn't have a lot of responsibility on our plate. I was semi-retired for a little bit and Hal was in-between businesses, so these two bachelors end up hanging out in Newport Beach. He'd call me in the morning and ask, "What are you doing?" I'd say, "Nothing." He'd say, "Let's go hit the gym." We'd hit the gym. We'd grab some lunch or breakfast. We'd hit the pool, go out for dinner, grab cigars, go to the yacht club, and pick up girls. We were the oddest couple. I was in my early 20s, he was in his late 60s or early 70s, but it didn't matter, because everybody loved Hal, young and old, because he was so magnanimous and so interesting. He always had such amazing stories, the kind of stories you can only get from life experience. We had a great time.

During that time, do you think I picked his brain? Of course I picked his brain! He was so giving and so gracious. The way I learned from him was through his stories. He used to tell me the most amazing stories of how he would pick up these companies, how he would get them for very little money or use a ton of leverage to do it. He would tell me about how once he cleaned them up he would finance them and take them public.

He would share stories with me every day, and every day I'd go home and write down the stories in my journal. After a while I began to see that there were patterns. As I saw these patterns I began to put together what I call my early eight keys to business success. It was just a concept at the time. When I put that together I went out to all my friends that weren't successful in business, and I had a lot of them back then. I asked them about their business process. There wasn't much of a process. Then I went out to my few friends that I had that were super successful, and there weren't a lot back then, but I had some. They did have a process. I began to see patterns.

I put together my early eight keys, and I've used those eight keys, as I've refined them over the decades, to create many business successes over the years. I attribute much of that success to Hal. That was my early experience with mentorship, and that encounter that summer changed the face of my entire life. I'm so grateful to have had that, especially at such a young age, because it gave me such a head start. I really love sharing that in a Mastermind and mentorship situation.

Taking It To The Next Level

We've been facilitating our New Wealth and Freedom Mastery Program since 2011, and we work with entrepreneurs to help them take their business to the next level. It's been a great program, but we wanted to help our clients achieve even better results. Early in 2015, we decided to redesign our program. We service clients in three different stages of entrepreneurship: 1) pre-launch (still deciding what to do); 2) launch and profit (those who are launching their business, product or service, setting up their platform; 3) those ready for accelerated growth and expansion via systems and joint ventures.

In Oct 2015 we launched Beyond Results Mastery, a program that includes strategy session, performance reviews, mastermind, accountability and coaching to service those entrepreneurs who are in the launch and profit stage of their entrepreneurial career. This March we will launch our next level program, the Mastery Retreats.

The Mastery Retreats will take place in my home. It will be a very small group of no more than 20 people, and we will work on each other's business to take it to an uber level. I really created this for a couple of reasons: First, I love Masterminding, and because I'm at a higher level I love to Mastermind with people at a higher level, and I love to Mastermind with people that make me look like a kid, because that's how you bring yourself up. That's how you learn the stuff you didn't even know you didn't know. Second, I wanted to have a place where as people graduate from our new Beyond Results Mastery program they've got a place to go to keep that progress moving forward, and to go from the next level to the uber level. I really want to be the catalyst for that and have our own property to make that happen.

We'll meet four times a year, beginning in mid-March of 2016. Our goal is to make sure that enough deals are put together that you at least make your total investment back, if not several times your investment, the very first time you come. You don't even have to think about that. At the end of the day a lot of our members are more interested in the camaraderie, but ROI is important, too. If you come to the event and get everything paid for the first time out, then you can just have a blast, so that is always the goal.

I believe that the keys to a great Mastermind are really two things. First, of course, are the people. If the people aren't amazing and synergistic, then nobody's going to win. If the room's not amazing nothing's going to happen. If the room is full of amazing, accomplished people you're half way there. If they're amazing, accomplished, and completely selfless and ready to give and help others, then you're there. Second, you really need facilitators that are going to be the catalyst for the connections.

What I mean by that is people in a Mastermind setting will connect, and they'll make deals, but a lot of times they may not. It's two parties that come together, but maybe one doesn't want to overstep the boundaries of the relationship, or maybe one's not good at connecting, and so our team of Beejal, Aaron Benjamin, and myself will work together to make sure that people are teamed up at the events and over the next couple of weeks following the event. This is really the secret sauce to making sure that people make the deals, that the ROI is there, that everybody has a great time. That really comes down to just having a team of people that are selecting the right people. We work on an application basis to make sure that everybody is a great fit for the community, a great fit for each other, and that they're going to accomplish their goals through the community. Then we work together to make sure that everybody makes those connections.

I'm very excited about both Beyond Results Mastery and the Mastery Retreats. I know there are other Masterminds out there, some are free, and in my experience and the feedback we've gotten, they are not very structured or effective, and they don't work on a long-term basis. People have to have skin in the game.

We make it very affordable. We charge the kind of money that people can certainly get an ROI from. We've sold programs that were in the $50,000-$65,000 range, and we've cut those. While I know people sell high-priced mastermind type programs, it's become all about how much can we charge, and get away with it! That type of business model no longer interested us. In our hearts we knew we could help our clients create better faster results from our program for a fraction of the investment. We wanted to create a coaching/mastermind program that provided all the benefits of programs 10 times the investment, and that's exactly what we've been able to do.

Today, our programs are very affordable. If you're in the early stage of business, about to launch a product or service, establishing your brand, struggling to create consistent results, need a marketing funnel, feeling overwhelmed and unproductive, going from event to event, investing in program after program and not seeing the results you desire, Beyond Results Mastery is the program for you. Go ahead and visit **www.BeyondMasteryRetreats.com** for more information.

If your business has been established, and you're ready for accelerated growth and prosperity, through implementation of high level business systems and joint ventures, then you're a potential candidate for the Mastery Retreats. To get more information on the program simply visit **www.MasteryRetreats.com** and fill out an application to see if you qualify. Regardless of which program is right for you, we look forward to working with you and taking you to the uber level.

About Daven Michaels

Daven Michaels presents innovative marketing strategies to entrepreneurs and business leaders all over the globe year after year. Aside from being a dynamic business and personal development trainer, he is the founder and CEO of 123Employee, the premiere outsourcing center in the Philippines, with hundreds of employees working thousands of hours per day for freedom-starved entrepreneurs worldwide.

Daven is also the brains behind the 'New Wealth & Freedom' system, while also being an in-demand speaker. In addition, he travels the globe educating entrepreneurs about the benefits of outsourcing and the importance of delegation.

Many personal development trainers talk about making more money, working less, turning your passion into prosperity, having more time and freedom, and many sell great info products. Daven does more than talk about it, though: he has lived it, breathes it, teaches his success formula and strategies, and through 123Employee services helps entrepreneurs all over the world make more money, save valuable time and create the lifestyle they dream about.

Daven Michaels has been labeled a 'Super Entrepreneur' by the media and his associates. Daven, who has been an entrepreneur since the age of 15, has enjoyed successful careers in the designer clothes retail industry, music promotion for crowds, and an award-winning career as a music and TV producer.

Daven models the lifestyle he inspires, managing hundreds of employees with only a laptop and an internet connection.

Now he devotes his energies to helping others discover the freedom of outsourcing as the CEO of 123Employee.

To connect with Daven and to learn more: **www.DavenMichales.com**

- 123Employee: **www.123Employee.com**
- Beyond Results Mastery: **www.BeyondResultsMastery.com**
- Mastery Retreats: **www.MasteryRetreats.com**

> *"I made my money the old-fashioned way. I was very nice to a wealthy relative right before he died."*
>
> ~Malcolm Forbes~

Chapter 7

10X Your Business in 22 Minutes

By Tom Beal

If you're like me, you like to cut right to the chase. That's exactly what I'm going to do here in this article. Let me ask you these 3 simple questions first:

1. Have you ever overcomplicated anything in your business?

2. Has anyone ever shared a tip or strategy with you that afterwards gave you an entirely new perspective and way of doing things?

3. Do you believe that it is possible to 10X your business in the upcoming year?

If you answered yes to any or all of those questions, you're going to love this chapter. It is my hope that this incredible process I'm going to share with you has the similar game & results changing impact for you as it has for the thousands of entrepreneurs I've shared it with this year alone in 11 different countries.

One in particular was a mastermind that had 12 people who invested $35,000.00 EACH to be a part of. After this process was explained to them and they went through it on day 1 of this 7 day mastermind, they all said that if this was all that they received in that week, it alone would be worth their investments. It was and is that much of a game changer.

Are you ready to learn it? Great! Here we go:

Step #1: Your Personal "You" Diagram

Have you ever seen an image that had a YOU in the middle of a sheet of paper then listed out an overwhelming amount of tasks and responsibilities that you were responsible for?

It was called The You Diagram, and creating your very own personal You Diagram is the start of this process and here's how to do it:

a. Grab a blank sheet of paper and a pen
b. Write down EVERY task, activity, and thing that you do on any given month related to your business
   I. Especially the Minimum Wage Activities that may even be embarrassing to yourself that you still do them
   II. Do NOT leave anything off of this list, write it all down

This has a twofold benefit for you, the first is to overwhelm you enough to have a recognition that, "this is CRAZY. I must make some changes if I want some changes in my results."

If you keep doing what you've been doing, you'll keep getting what you've been getting.

If nothing changes, nothing changes.

We'll discuss the 2nd benefit shortly in an upcoming step.

Step #2: Answer These 4 Questions (in The Specified Manner)

1. *What ONE THING do I need to start doing that has the potential to 10 X my business & results?*
   a. This answer is unique to you and your business, and the answer for many is something like: Webinars, Write a Book, Live Events, Product Launch, Create a New Product or Service, etc.

   b. The KEY is to choose ONE answer to this question being something that you are not currently doing in your business, but if and when you did start, it has the highest potential to dramatically boost your results by 10X.

What do I need to do more of? (My 3 Unique Abilities)
To answer this, pull out your You Diagram you completed in Step 1, and ask yourself this, "If I was only allowed to do 3 of these activities in the upcoming months, what would those 3 activities be?"

a. These are the 3 things that only you can do, that are the answer to "What is the absolute best use of my time, right now?" Many call this your Unique Abilities or Highest Revenue Producing Activities.

b. For me as a consultant mine are: Fulfilling Client Promises (individual & group consulting), Planting Seeds of Value In My Marketplace (Marketing), Product & Service Creation (Product & Funnel Completion then Product Launch)

c. Goal here is to get SUPER CLEAR on what the 3 best use of your time activities are, and to schedule them into your calendar more.

What do I need to do less of?
Grab your You Diagram again. The answer to this question is everything else except the answers from question #2.

a. Obviously, not all have the staff or resources when reading this to magically make all of these other tasks and responsibilities disappear immediately. However, now that you know what the best use of your time is and what isn't, NOW is the time to begin thinking about & creating systems, processes, outsourcing, and hiring to remove these non-essential tasks from your plate so you can focus more on your Unique Abilities.

What do I need to stop doing altogether?
All entrepreneurs have some "demons" or habits that are contrary to their desired goals, and you are no exception. This is a time for you to recognize that some of your habits and actions of the past

that may have served you in some way or fashion in the past no longer serve you and you are choosing to leave them behind as you grow internally and grow your results externally.

These 4 questions can be inserted into 4 quadrants of a square, to be remembered more easily, and applied by you regularly; not only to grow your business results, but for all areas of your life (health, relationships, and finances).

Jim Rohn says, "Things that are easy to do are easier not to do." …and is what separates the top performers from the rest. They do the small tasks that matter, while the rest don't.

I am confident that you would not have read this far, to drop the ball without implementing these simple steps. As Nike says, "Just do it!"

CAUTION: Don't let this process simplicity fool you. When you choose to go through it now and every few weeks, it can and will change everything for you, most importantly your profits and growth; internally & externally.

Do yourself, your results, and your peace of mind a favor and actually do this process NOW, then create a plan to follow through with the answers to those 4 questions:

1. START that one thing which has the highest potential to 10X your business when completed and implemented.
2. DO MORE of your unique abilities, which are the absolute highest and best use of your time.
3. DO LESS of minimum wage activities. Create systems, processes, and staff that allows these to be off of your plate.
4. STOP DOING the things that are counter to the goals you have stated.

BONUS TIP: Have each one of your team members go through this process, as well, and watch their clarity, productivity, and results skyrocket, along with your business results.

About Tom Beal

Tom Beal is an international speaker, author, and consultant who is a master in assisting his clients in simplifying their success, results, and lives. He is the creator of The Success Magnet System, The Trinity Success Method, and book to be released in 2016 titled, "S.O.S.: Stop Overcomplicating Success."

After being born to teenagers, raised around 4 divorces & 6 marriages, going to 9 different schools by 8th grade, and raised on welfare...

Tom was able to become a National Bicycle Champion, the #1 Honor Graduate in Marine Corps Boot Camp at Parris Island, recipient of 3 meritorious promotions in 4 years while in the Marine Corps, #1 in 5 sales organizations, Publisher of The North Carolina Home Book, and President of Kelly-Media, Inc (a Jim Kelly - NFL HOF QB company), side by side with Mike Filsaime from 2006-2011, producing over $20 million in online results, and President of Strategic Profits for Rich Schefren for 2.5 years, from 2011-2013, then Founder of Make Today Great podcast.

In 2015 alone, Tom traveled to 11 countries and shared game changing strategies and trainings to 1,000's of entrepreneurs and his message for you today is:

"It doesn't matter where you came from, or where you are right now, there are steps you can take TODAY to begin turning your dreams into reality; personally and professionally."

Feeling stressed, overwhelmed, and ready to bring your results to a whole new level? Tom is a master at assisting you in reaching your next level, regardless of obstacles or roadblocks that have prevented you from breaking through the plateau you've reached, up to this point.

Stop Overcomplicating Success and go take your Success Intake NOW to begin the process of turning your dreams into reality at:

http://tombeal.com/successintake

NOTE: This is normally reserved as a 1st step for all of Tom's clients, but he wanted to share it with you here today at no charge, to dramatically impact your trajectory IMMEDIATELY!

> *"Not everything that can be counted counts, and not everything that counts can be counted."*
>
> ~Albert Einstein~

Chapter 8

Put Your Trust In Me

By Lou Brown

Hi my name Lou Brown. I've been Buying, Selling and Holding property for more than 30 years. Along the way I discovered THE most powerful yet little understood entity on the Planet.

It's called Trusts. I discovered about 30 different benefits of trusts that you can't get with any other entity! Not only can Trusts change your life, unlike other entities, they can serve you after death.

Trusts are the absolute solution for anyone interested in long term wealth, because you can make it, but the question is, can you keep it? It's so easy for someone, particularly in this country, to come along and take everything you've got, only because you failed to protect yourself. It's simple, and it's easy, and it can be done yourself. It doesn't have to be a complicated, drawn out, or expensive process.

To me the true path to wealth is when you have dependable, predictable monthly income, and the very best way I've found that works is to have something that everyone needs, which is a home to live in. That exists. With well-located real estate there is always going to be a demand. It's never going to go out of style, and it's always going to produce a monthly dividend, unlike the stock market, which can go up and down. Certainly real estate can go up and down, but what doesn't tend to change very much is the rental income, and in fact in today's market it's going up dramatically. So it's a dependable, predictable monthly income for anyone.

Rent year in and year out over the history of the US has always been about 1/3 of a person's income, no matter whether the markets are up or down or sideways. That's the typical amount of money a person can comfortably spend on housing without getting in trouble.

If you own three free and clear houses, that pretty much will support you in your particular level of lifestyle. Based on the type of lifestyle that you're looking for, just add more properties. Owning rental properties can be boring and unexciting, most of the time, but it also happens to be extremely self-sustaining. As much as people want to do something else a bit more interesting, the challenge is that those interesting things often change, and they really don't have a big future. With rental real estate you can do better.

In our program we teach you to take advantage of and address all the issues with long term ownership of property. One of the big issues is when people don't pay. We address that. We do payroll deduction. Another issue is when people aren't motivated to pay. We address that with our Path to Home Ownership program, where we're giving our tenants, regardless of background or credit, the opportunity to end up with ownership of a property.

Trust Protection

One of the issues we seek to address is the fact that people will take advantage of people that own property, people that have assets, so we don't make them easily, readily available. With the use of a trust, which can be created at the moment of time that an asset is acquired, they are hidden from view and no one can see what someone actually owns.

Nothing should be owned in your personal name. Not your bank account, vehicles, stocks, bonds, mutual funds or your company. Any rental property you own should be in a trust.

Can setting up a trust be done on your own, or do you need a professional? Let me address that by saying you're about to bury your bones, and this is an area you should not do without full knowledge, and I really do believe that. This is where people get screwed up.

I've got a situation right now where a friend of mine passed away. Because he did take a trust training course and he put his assets in a trust, his girlfriend became the beneficiary of the trust. As they weren't married his family should have inherited his estate. She would have gotten absolutely nothing had he not done it that way.

The nice thing, a Trust doesn't even have to go into probate.

Entity Nightmares

Attorneys can make a whole lot more money when they advise you to use something they do understand and can set up for you, such as Limited Liability Companies (LLCs), Corporations or Family Limited Partnerships.

One of the plans attorneys typically suggest is to put everything in one LLC, or one corporation. They say that will give you asset protection. Seems like a brilliant idea... Then one day BOOM! That corporation or LLC, the owner of the property, gets sued and now everything is at risk because it was all owned by a single entity. That was a very bad plan because while you personally had protection, your properties had none! Wouldn't you agree?

Now you're concerned about each asset, as you should be. When you ask the attorneys what to do, they say, "If you're so worried about liability, why don't you get an LLC for each house?" Another brilliant idea. (NOT!) Now, we've got annual dues to pay, annual fees to pay, annual tax returns to do, a separate bank account for each LLC and in some states like Maryland, there's an extra annual fee of $300 per entity. In California it's even worse: $800 per entity! They also don't mention that these types of entities are going to cost you a lot to operate. Of course, the attorneys will have job security because you'll need them to explain all the things they didn't tell you – and they'll bill you for that, too! So, I don't think this is a Street Smart® plan for us. Do you?

I've been called lots of things over the years – "The King of Cash Flow," "The King of Forms," "The King of Trusts," among others. In fact, people really don't know what to call me, or what niche to put me in because the information and Tools I've developed are so broad-based and complete. I'd be happy with the "King of Systems for Real Estate Investing."

Ladies and gentlemen, truthfully, I don't know of anyone in the United States or anywhere in the world who teaches what I teach. More importantly, I know of no one who has a clear-cut, step-by-step system that takes you through the processes and procedures of exactly how to get wealthy using all the profit centers available in this great real estate business. Even if you've invested thousands in other education and so-called systems, as my licensees will attest, you will find that this is the system that will truly bring it all together for you. What's more, I fully guarantee it so you can see for yourself. How can you go wrong? What I'm sharing with you is not available anywhere else at any price.

Imagine this: We even have a system for teaching you the system! The overview of the entire system is taught at a three-day training called Millionaire Jump Start™.

We teach a lot more at our four-day trainings. We call them our in-depth trainings. "Buying Right" is taught at Millionaire Deal Maker™ (MDM) where attendees actually bring live leads that are worked and negotiated in group settings right in class. You also learn thirty-five different types of offers to make, no matter what situation or lead comes your way. You graduate as a Certified Deal Specialist™ (CDS) and receive specialized exclusive software to print out four different offers you can present to the seller without having to do all the paperwork. It does it for you.

"Selling and Holding Right" is taught in-depth at Massive Passive Income™ (MPI) where you learn how to manage right, build a portfolio for wealth, and to sell right, without competition or high selling costs. This one is critical if you plan to hold property. You also learn, in-depth, all of my varied exit strategies, so you are not approaching the market to sell with only one option, like other investors do. You graduate a Certified Income Specialist™ (CIS) and receive specialized exclusive software that does all your selling and renting paperwork for you along with proprietary calculators and other existing strategy support.

"Protecting Right" is taught at Maximum Asset Shield™ (MAS) where you actually bring your own deed(s) to class and right there we create your Land Trust for your real estate, your Personal Property Trust for your vehicles, stocks, bank account, etc. and we create your Living Trust for all your wealth to be protected and have tax benefits, too! You leave with your estate plan done and you actually know what happened! You graduate a Certified Trust Specialist™ (CTS) and receive specialized exclusive software that does all your Trust paperwork for you, along with your all-important "Subject-to" paperwork.

As you grow your business, we support you with advanced training known as Mastering Business Advancement™ where you learn how to hire staff and truly build a multi-million dollar business the right way. You'll graduate as an MBA and receive proprietary software for that next level of your business advancement as well.

Hey, what did they teach you in college? How to work for someone else?! Our intensive program is designed to get you to the money faster and safer, and to keep you in the business for years to come.

Some of you are asking, "What do I need to do next?" The answer is: Get started! You need the Tools to really have what it takes to capture the profits and protect yourself. Some of you will be ready to get the full program of Tools, Training, Technology and Team. You will be rewarded with a greater discount when you get everything.

Frankly, we have found that our most successful licensees start with the full system A Franchise Without The Cost™, what we call the Total Package™. We have a financing plan and can make this painless to get you on the right track. Others of you don't have the budget or the credit to make that work. For you, we have the Whole Enchilada®, Jr. to get you going towards quick profits. Doesn't it make sense for you to take action now so you will have what you know is right for your success? This is your chance to make the money in this business that you deserve for yourself and your family. And it's out there waiting for you. Call now 1-800-578-8580. You are doing the right thing.

To Your Profits!

P. S.

Spend some time to learn how to keep what you've earned. This is not an area that you need to just write a check. This is an area that you need to pay attention. This is an area that you need to master and have full knowledge of, because it's so easy for someone else to take it from you, especially when you're not there to protect it.

About Lou Brown

Investors have long regarded the training, systems and forms created by **Louis "Lou" Brown** as the best in the industry. Quoted as an expert by many publications such as *The Wall Street Journal* and *Smart Money,* Lou draws from his wide and varied background as a real estate investor. Having bought property since 1977, he has invested in single-family homes, apartments, hotels and developed subdivisions, as well as building and renovating homes and apartments. These experiences have given him a proving ground for the most cutting edge concepts in the real estate investment industry today. He is widely known as a creative financing genius regarding his deal structuring concepts. He enjoys sharing his discoveries with others as he teaches seminars and has authored courses, books and audio training on how to make money and keep it.

Lou is past President and a lifetime member of Georgia Real Estate Investors Association and was founding President of the National Real Estate Investors Association. He firmly believes that the path to success is through ongoing education, and invests thousands of dollars annually in his own.

Lou loves to spend time in Atlanta with his beautiful wife Janice, their two children and foster daughter, and he always makes time to speak with other realtors and investors about his *Street Smart* and *Path to*

Traffic and Conversion Mastery

Homeownership programs.

So if you are interested in learning how Lou can take you to the next level, then visit his website at **www.louisbrown.com** or contact him directly at **StreetSmartLouis@LouisBrown.com**.Street Smart Systems, LLC.

Chapter 9

The WOW! Strategy™ - The Key To Solving ALL Of Your Sales And Marketing Problems

By Steve Sipress

Have you ever been an "advertising victim?" That means you had an advertising sales rep make all kinds of claims and promises, so you signed the contract and paid your bill – but then the ad just didn't work? Good news! I have a solution to that problem.

Do you not have effective marketing systems in place in your business, so you're always wondering where your next customer is going to come from? Good news! You're about to find a solution to that.

Are you getting beat up by competitors – some that are much bigger and better-funded than you – so you end up lowering your fee or price, and you think you don't really have a chance of competing with them? Again, you're about to have a solution for that problem.

Are you ever seen as a commodity, where your prospects think you're just the same as your competitors, with no compelling differentiation – you're "just another" doctor, lawyer, plumber, or whatever you are – so you think you've got to compete on price? Congratulations, there's a solution to that.

Did you ever read a book, or watch a video, or attend a seminar, and you hear all kinds of great ideas about marketing, and then you get back to your office and you realize: "I don't even know where to start – I don't know how to implement any of this stuff?" Great news! You're about to have a solution to that.

How about cold calling? Do you or your sales staff still do that and get nothing but miserable, demotivating, non-results?

Do you ever try to sell to tire-kickers and time-wasters who only say things like "Sure. Sounds great. Work up a proposal and get back to me in a few weeks" or "Can you just send me some information?"

Do you ever encounter price-shoppers, who always want to talk you down on your price or fee?

Do you ever try to sell to people who have no respect for you, won't listen to you, and won't even let you in the door, even though you know you can help them out? They look down on you and don't see you as an equal or as a valuable resource?

Congratulations, you're about to have a solution to all of these problems.

Why Traditional Marketing Doesn't Work For Small Businesses

Let me start by telling you what I'm *not* going to give you as a solution.

I am *not* going to tell you to just spend money to "get your name out there," or to put your name on a blimp, or to put your logo on a NASCAR, or name a stadium, or any nonsense like that where you're paying to get some warm and fuzzy feelings about yourself, or your brand, or your company, or your product, or your service. That's *not* what I'm going to tell you to do.

What I *am* going to tell you about is called "direct response marketing," which means that you're actually going to get paid to "get your name out there." That's right – you're going to make money every time someone hears about your business.

Let me ask you a question: Have you ever heard of the "ShamWOW!®?"

If you have, think about it: Was it because of the ShamWOW!® blimp? The ShamWOW!® NASCAR? The ShamWOW!® Stadium?

Of course not.

A couple of years ago, direct response marketing ads for it were playing non-stop all over TV, the internet, and all kinds of other places. That means that every time you saw a ShamWOW!®, it was being sold. The ShamWOW!® company was making money every time you heard about it. In other words, they made money every time they built their brand.

That's what direct response marketing is. You never have to pay to build your brand or "get your name out there."

Another way to think about direct response marketing is that you're "cutting out the middleman" – you're going directly to your prospects to get an *immediate* response to whatever it is you're offering.

Let me ask you a question: Do you happen to have a chain of stores all throughout your chosen market, that are all filled with highly-paid, highly-trained, highly-motivated salespeople, so that all you have to do is get people to have a warm and fuzzy feeling and some general "awareness" about your company, so that when they see your products on a shelf in a store, they might buy from you?

For those of us who don't have that kind of army of mass distribution going on all around, we've got to make the sale ourselves. We've got to sell directly to the consumer. We don't have any "middleman" to sell our stuff for us.

That's why we can't copy what we see big companies doing when it comes to the marketing of our goods and services. Because we're small business owners, we have a *much* tougher job to do with our marketing, and we need to be at the top of our game.

We do not have an army of highly-skilled, highly-paid, highly-motivated salespeople populating stores throughout the country, ready to sell our products and services for us, so that all we have to do is create some warm and fuzzy feelings and stay "top of mind" among our prospects.

Our advertising has to do double-duty: We have to display and describe what we're selling, but then we also have to actually *sell* it, too.

A Few Examples

Car manufacturers often show little more than photos of their cars and trucks in their ads – sometimes adding only a word or two, like "Tough" or "Zoom Zoom."

Local car dealerships could never survive if they did that. Their ads show images of cars, but they must also be full of reasons to buy, and buy NOW – discount prices, easy credit, flexible terms, etc. And think about the television commercials of local car dealerships. Those include some of the most outrageous and memorable attention-getting antics of the dealership owners themselves, using their personalities to stand out from their competition and *sell cars.* I don't remember seeing any big car company executives in *any* of their ads since Lee Iacocca over 30 years ago.

Liquor manufacturers can show just their bottles in their ads, with almost no words on the page (in fact, Absolut has won awards and was voted into the Marketing Hall of Fame in 1995 for doing just that).

Local liquor stores need to run ads listing the brand names they carry – but also their prices, hours, location, and most important of all, special sales, discounts and other incentives to buy *now.*

Sporting equipment manufacturers can just use their logo and slogan as their entire advertisement. *Local* sporting goods store owners can't Just Do That.

A photo of a diamond with a simple slogan might be great for a big diamond company, but a *local* jewelry store owner has to include plenty of details about its rings, necklaces, etc. – including, of course, "special limited time" deals.

And so on, and so on. I think you get the idea.

Small business owners' advertising and marketing is not about looking pretty, or being entertaining, or winning awards. We can do all of that if we want, but not at the expense of our main goal: *To sell something. Now.*

That's what *we're* all about as small business owners – our pay isn't based on stock prices or what anyone thinks about our company. That's why we can't do what the big companies do. We need to use direct response marketing, and *sell*.

Two Big Breakthroughs

Now that you're starting to "get it," it's time for you to make two Big Breakthroughs.

The first one is to decide that you are not in the "deliverable" business – whatever product or service you happen to deliver. You're no longer an attorney, or a doctor, or a plumber, or a carpet cleaner.

From this point forward, you are now in the business of *marketing* your business.

Here's why that makes a big difference…

I'm going to assume that you provide an excellent product or service. But does that mean that you also necessarily have excellent revenue and profits? Of course not. It's just the ante to get into the game. Once you provide an excellent product or service, then you have to implement effective marketing to gain customers, clients or patients.

Think about it: If you improve your already-excellent product or service a little more, is that going to double or triple your income this year? Of course not. What you've got to do now is to get your marketing going. THAT can double or triple your income – or more! – in a VERY short time.

So that's the first Big Breakthrough: If you're an attorney, you're not a lawyer anymore – you're in the business of marketing legal services. And so on. It's a mindset breakthrough – the first and most important one you'll make if you really want to transform your income and lifestyle.

Now here's your second Big Breakthrough: Since you've now decided that you are a marketer of products or services, instead of just a doer or provider of something, from now on you're going to focus most of your time and energy on implementing effective marketing – or you're going to get the right team in place to do it.

Who do YOU have on your team to implement effective marketing for *your* business?

Traditional vs. Direct Response Marketing

Traditional marketing is really nothing more than "spraying and praying" – trying to attack everyone with your message, and forcing yourself on disinterested people. It's an ugly, uphill, unpleasant battle.

Much better is to have your ideal prospects open their doors, roll out the red carpet, and welcome you, inviting you to sell to them by saying, "What do you got?" That's direct response marketing.

Traditional marketing is throwing mud against the wall and seeing what sticks. Direct response marketing is putting out money, and getting more money back – quickly, and with all results trackable. It is not just "getting your name out there" with branding and slogans and logos, and all that kind of general stuff.

Traditional marketing is a really bad model for the business owner, because the advertising sales rep gets paid whenever they sell an ad – even if the phone never rings for the business owner. You can't depend on advertising sales reps to help you place effective ads (I know, because I used to be one). That's not their strength – selling ad space is. Direct response marketing ads don't win awards for looking pretty – they just generate results.

Traditional marketing is basically rolling the dice. As all-time business great John Wanamaker once famously said, "Half the money I spend on advertising is wasted, and the trouble is I don't even know which half." In other words, with traditional advertising you really have no idea what the heck is going on. I don't know about you, dear reader, but I cannot afford to be wasting my advertising dollars and not even knowing which of my ads, if any, are actually working to make me money.

I've been there and done that in my own businesses, many years ago, so I know the feeling. But never again.

The Small Business Owner's Best Friend

Some 50 years ago, David Ogilvy, one of the all-time advertising geniuses, said, "Only the mail order people know what they're doing." He hated it when his advertising sales reps brought him crappy "branding" ads that looked nice but didn't generate concrete results for the advertiser.

Today, direct response marketing takes many different forms – not just "mail order" advertising. Anytime you see an infomercial, or an ad offering some kind of education such as a free report, or a home shopping channel, you're seeing direct response marketing in action.

When done correctly, direct response marketing makes your actual selling efforts much easier (and, in many cases, all you have to do is take orders, because your marketing is *that* effective).

Another great thing about direct response marketing: Since it doesn't involve all kinds of pretty or funny creativity, it's extremely easy to model your own marketing off of other companies' effective direct response marketing and ads.

Remember: This is *not* about entertaining, or being cute, or making funny Super Bowl ads, or winning awards for "creativity." It's about getting *results*. As David Ogilvy said, "We sell, or else." Direct response marketing is not about entertainment, or art, or humor. It's about making *sales*. Period.

Okay. So now you know *why* to use direct response marketing. Here's *how* to make it work for you and your business...

The WOW! Strategy™ - Three Simple Steps To Success

The first "W" stands for the "WHO." For your marketing to be effective, WHO you're selling to is always more important than WHAT you're selling.

You need to zero in on your ideal target market. Make it your business to know everything about them – what they want, what they don't want, exactly who they are and how they think, act and feel. Once you really dig deep and do this, you will be able to attract your ideal clients, and repel the potential clients that you don't want at the same time.

After you figure out everything you can about your ideal WHO, you need to determine whether or not they are "reachable." Where do they "hang out" – both online and offline? What publications do they read, what TV shows do they watch, what groups do they belong to? You need to choose a WHO which is both big enough in size and economically realistic enough for you to engage, so that you can bring in the revenue and profits you desire.

Next is the "O," which is your Irresistible "OFFER" – one your target market absolutely loves, and cannot refuse. You've got to put in a ton of time, research and brainpower to come up with that, because this one element alone can revolutionize your business, and, in fact, your entire industry.

"Take Any 11 Records or Tapes for One Penny" (and then a couple of selections at regular price later on) made millions of dollars for the Columbia Record and Tape Club, and sent thousands of record stores scrambling to try to compete with them. That OFFER was completely irresistible to millions of music fans.

Not sure how to create your own Irresistible OFFER? Guarantee something. If you own a pizza parlor near a college campus, so that your ideal WHO is a pot-smoking student who can't drive when he has the munchies, you just say, "I'll bring a pizza right to you, hot and quick. Guaranteed."

*WARNING: When you have a guarantee, make sure you can follow through. And do the math to figure out how many people are likely to take you up on your guarantee, compared to the many additional customers, clients or patients you will attract because of it.

The final "W" stands for the "WAY" or "WAYS" that you use to get your OFFER to your WHO. It's as simple as that. There's no such thing as a "good" or "bad" WAY in general; no matter what anyone tells you, you can make plenty of money using any conceivable method of advertising or marketing (or else they wouldn't exist). It's simply a matter of figuring out which WAY or WAYS are the most appropriate for your chosen WHO to receive your OFFER.

Notice that I didn't say it's what is most appropriate for *you* or what *your* favorite choice is or what *you* want to use. That's a huge mistake that many business owners make. They come to me and ask, "Can you help me build an effective website?" or "Can you help me market my business on the internet?" or "Can you help me with social media?"

Of course I can help any business owner advertise and market their business using any of those WAYS – and a whole lot more, as well. But that's the completely backwards way to go about it. You need to choose your WAY or WAYS based on which one or ones your WHO is most likely to receive and respond to your OFFER.

So if you're selling wheelchairs or canes or "I've fallen and I can't get up" services to seniors, you wouldn't be silly enough to use text messages in your marketing – even if that's what *you* would like to use. And if you have a pizza place located across the street from a high school, you wouldn't send direct mail to all of the students to let them know about your "Free Slice Of Pizza With Purchase Of Any Drink For The First 25 Kids Who Come In Within The Next Hour" special. I think you get the point.

If you're experiencing any problems with your sales or marketing, it's simply because you aren't properly using one, or two, or all three of the elements of The WOW! Strategy™. Get all three of these areas working properly in your business, and watch your revenue and profits skyrocket!

About Steve Sipress

Steve Sipress is a successful serial entrepreneur, who has created and built over a dozen successful companies of his own, while helping thousands of other ambitious and aggressive business owners, entrepreneurs, executives and sales professionals all around the world do the same over the past 35+ years.

He has assembled a team of the world's top business-building experts as the publisher of *Rhino Monthly Magazine,* the *RhinoDaily.com blog* and the *Rhino Daily Podcast*. He has written numerous newsletters and articles on sales and marketing for a wide range of publications, has appeared on radio, television and in international media, is the best-selling author of several books, and is widely recognized as one of the world's top experts in helping small business owners explode their revenue and profits with effective direct response marketing strategies and tactics.

He has won many awards for both marketing and sales, and he is the creator of The WOW Strategy™: The Key To Helping Small Business Owners Solve All Of Their Sales And Marketing Problems.

Want a dramatic transformation of your own business? Take advantage of a free 1-on-1 Strategy Session with Steve by going to: **www.HelpFromSteve.com**

"Persist – don't take no for an answer. If you're happy to sit at your desk and not take any risk, you'll be sitting at your desk for the next 20 years."

~David Rubenstein~

Chapter 10

The Case Against Making A Windfall of Money

By Matt Bacak

Many people get destroyed after making a windfall of money because they have no idea what's about to happen to them.

However, there's a reason that they can't handle the sudden windfall - they are doing it all wrong!

This chapter reveals 5 tips for what to do when you suddenly make a crap load of cold hard cash..

Before I get deeper into this subject, let me ask you a silly question....

Question: When do most people buy their alarm systems?

Answer: After they get robbed.

I asked you that silly question because you want to read every word in this chapter so you don't get screwed since the average entrepreneur cycles (gets their butt handed to them) 2-3 times.

Here's another question that will set the stage for this chapter.

What drives your Goal, your Why?

It may be proving yourself or proving someone wrong, it might be the desire to never worry about where your next meal is coming from.

But attached to what drives you are the list of things that will confirm to you that you have arrived.

For me, it was reaching the status of millionaire before age 30. It was also tied to my goal of becoming a pilot and owning an airplane, having a big office and staff, living in "the" neighborhood. I could justify all these things as good investments because a plane and a house are assets, right? And a big staff means making more money than just a small team could, right?

Actually, no.

Things that require expensive upkeep and monthly fees like an airplane and hanger are, in truth, liabilities. Same is true for boats and high-end cars. And a big staff is a big payroll in the bad months, and even in the good months, more revenue is not more profit. Revenue is all the money coming in, the number that businesses love to boast. But profit is what you have after expenses and a million in revenue with 50% expense ratio is a lot more work and stress than $600,000 minus $100,000 expenses, even though your net profit is the same.

When you do crack the code, I urge you to have the long term, not the fantasies of your childhood push you. Financial success brings hangers-on, the ones that get you to buy them drinks and expensive toys that you keep up while they play for free.

Most people see rock stars and star athletes and think, if I ever got my hands on money like that I would be set for life. Don't they see it won't last? Just as athletes have a limited season for getting the big contracts and injury is an obvious possibility, when you are on top of your game, you feel invincible. And the people around you think you are invincible. I mean if you figured out how to make a million once, you can do it again, right? If your write a hit song, a second hit is easy right?

One of the reasons we are all prone to spending like it will never end is being caught in the flow like a gambler.

Here are 5 tips for what to do when you suddenly make a crap load of cold hard cash:

1. Hire a fee-only financial planner (actually do this when you get past breaking even)
2. Don't spend it all – it isn't all really yours (refund, taxes)
3. A sudden windfall will amplify, not change who you are. Happy – happier. Angry – angrier
4. Keep it on the down low, otherwise everyone will want something from you
5. Hold on to your money – just enjoy seeing it in your bank account while you make good decisions

How do you get ready now? Have systems and rules in place. Every 6 months go through your bills, especially on Paypal or your credit card and purge things you aren't using. Start investing this money automatically every month.

Realize that you need percentage allocations for everything above your hard expenses and you should keep those very low. Something like monthly living and office expenses and taxes equals $10,000. When you earn $50,000 one month, first create an emergency fund with 3 months expenses, then with the remaining $10,000 30% for retirement, 10% in marketing, rest divided between fun goals and instant gratification. If you make $50,000 again next month, you have $40,000 to divide up like that.

I was the kid that created a list of all the things that would make me feel rich and important – airplane, traveling the world and a big office. I hung out with gurus who bragged about their revenue, their cars and vacations. And the more I listened the more I fed this cycle of stuff that I wasn't buying for me, I was buying it for them. I stopped owning my stuff and it owned me. It made me work 80 hours a week or more. It made me travel or be in classes with clients more than I was home. It took my health. I was lost and drowning until I finally took my wife's advice.

Which was...

Follow the 5 tips.

Matt Bacak

P.S. You're probably wondering why a fee-only planner. Well, fee-only financial planners are registered investment advisors with a fiduciary responsibility to act in their clients' best interest. They do not accept any fees or compensation based on product sales. Fee-only advisors have fewer inherent conflicts of interest, and they generally provide more comprehensive advice.

P.S. Don't be as stubborn as I was. If you would like a referral to my personal financial planner, I'd be glad to put you in contact with her. Simply email me at **mattbacak@gmail.com.**

About Matt Bacak

Matt Bacak is considered by many an Internet Marketing Legend. Using his stealth marketing techniques, he became a Best Selling author with a huge fan base of over 1.2 million people in his niche, as well as built multi-million dollar companies.

After being crowned 2010 Internet Marketer of the Year, he was asked to appear on National Television, his Lifetime television segment focused on "how to make money using the Internet. The real way".

Matt is not only a sought-after internet marketer but has also marketed for some of the world's top experts whose reputations would shrivel if their followers ever found out someone else coached them on their online marketing strategies.

To see if Matt can help you though your journey, simply email him at **mattbacak@gmail.com.**

It's easy to make a buck. It's a lot tougher to make a difference.

~Tom Brokaw~

Chapter 11

Sponsoring A Successful Event

By Sheila Farragher-Gemma

As I look back on my childhood, it's really not surprising that connecting people comes naturally to me. Many nights as we sat around the dinner table the conversation would turn to someone's kid that had just graduated with a degree (in Hotel Management, for example) and my Mom would immediately ask my Dad "Mick, who do we know in the Hotel industry? I know! Peter Cullen at Ashford. I'll call him in the morning" And presto, someone's unsuspecting daughter just had her career launched!

When I started what I like to call my first info business, I really had no idea that there was a whole big world out there of information marketing and events, but I was lucky to get introduced to it early on. One thing I realized very early on was that I was good at making connections and seeing opportunity between two business people before they quite saw it for themselves. In every business I have owned, I was always the one who created strategic partnerships, the person who created joint ventures. It was through this medium that I met a fabulous lady, DeAnna Rogers, and started to work closely with her to create a forum where people like us could meet, exchange ideas and do business with each other.

Since we worked so well together, DeAnna and I decided to do what we did best, joint venture, and started a business together called Affiliate Mastermind Group. This was basically a company that was a support system for people who were involved in information marketing and wanted to leverage doing joint ventures together. We would meet a couple times a year and do events to open up that networking. From there we ran our own AMG events as well, which in essence became my first introduction to doing sponsorships.

We were quickly noticed and it wasn't long before the owners of Digital Marketer started to woo DeAnna to come work for their company. They eventually made her an offer she couldn't refuse and she took over as their Director of Events. She quickly realized that she didn't have anyone handling sponsorship. What she needed was someone who could take over the project and own it, so she had contacted me to see if I'd be interested in doing it, and I said of course I would. I started helping her out with that, and in the process other people in the industry started seeing what I was doing and asked if I could help them with their events as well.

After doing a few sponsorships for AMG and other non-related events, and now with Digital Marketer, I actually found that I liked what I was doing.

I knew a lot of people in the industry and I knew what would work for people in terms of sponsorship. Sponsorship goes a lot farther than just having somebody come in, pay you a bunch of money, you give them a table and say thanks. I looked at the people that came to the events as someone I could really help in terms of sponsorship, so I asked them to come in and be a sponsor, which most did. We had to make sure that the alliance fed both sides. That's the importance of building something long term versus just a quick shot of money into your event.

I found that it was easier to find sponsors when you had the right audience for them. It's like anything in sales: you have to think of it from the point of view of the other person. What's in it for them? You're constantly in that "what's in it for them" type of mindset, so you need to give them something that brings a lot of value and is a no-brainer for them.

Let's take our last AMG event as an example. As we were fortunate to have a huge number of sponsors, we decided to shake things up a little bit and do something that was practically unheard of. We asked the sponsors if they would be willing to set up work stations where our attendees could come over and not only find out about the Sponsors business, but also get to use his product in their own business and get some of the ideas and strategies they were learning about that weekend implemented. Now the sponsors were no longer just standing behind a booth handing out business cards. They ran mini workshops where the people attending the event could go over and not only meet the sponsors and listen to what they had to say, but also get a quick head shot with a photographer or a quick outline idea from one of our book publishing companies or watch a demo of how Infusionsoft could automate their business.

What we wanted was for the attendee to come away not only with some great content from the weekend, but with some of those ideas they had heard or strategies they had learnt, already implemented. For example, they created a business plan, or mapped out a marketing plan, whatever the particular workshop was. It gave the attendee a great taste of who the Sponsor was and they generally continued to do business with them long after the event. We found that that worked out very well for everyone.

Sponsorship is an easy thing to seek out, because everyone looks at this as a way to get a bunch of money into their events. However, there is a lot more to it than that. I found I have to be picky when deciding who I work will with. It's really important to me that this person has a serving attitude when it comes to their sponsors. I've seen events where all the sponsor booths were practically in a different ballroom in a hotel in a different city! They never see any traffic. It's really important that if you partner with a company to sponsor your event that you really work hard to ensure that they get the best bang for their buck and have every single opportunity to a make a return on their investment.

Being Credible

Adding named sponsors helps from a credibility standpoint to bring more people into the event. However, when you are starting out, sometimes you have to give a lot away to attract the types of sponsors you are looking for. The onus is on you to prove the value of your event, and once you have achieved that they will return year after year.

I took all the systems that I originally built for myself and I modified them to work with Digital Marketer, and I eventually modified them so that I am able to work with any promoter and any event, including one of my best, Traffic and Conversion. It's always a fluid thing. Every event is different. Every sponsorship has different needs. There has to be a lot of flexibility so that you can really work with a company to make sure that they are getting what they need while keeping within the integrity of the event.

The business I have built helps me identify the connections that make sense and to nurture those connections while building strong, long-lasting mutually beneficial relationships between promoter and sponsor. This is not impossible for a promoter to do on his own. However, where I bring the value is not only from my experience, but with my ability to take the ball and run with it, freeing the promoter to be able to focus on all of the other aspects of his event that need his attention. If a sponsor has an issue, I make sure it is handled and that the event runs smoothly for everyone. That's the beauty of what I do. I literally take over that piece for them and just handle it.

Another benefit for the promoter is that it takes them out of that uncomfortable position of having to be the salesman and ask vendors and colleagues to pay for a sponsorship. It is a lot easier to pass that off to a third party much like in a negotiation. A lot of the time the person sponsoring has become a friend of the promoter and you need that middle person to get the job done in a neutral sensitive way.

Relationship Building

Remember that an event is all about relationship building rather than sales building. That will come. This is the time for one-on-one bonding. Genuinely get to know perspective clients. Get to know their business, what their needs are. You want to build relationships so that people who are ready to buy will buy, but when you go back to the office and you call up Mike, you want to remember something significant about Mike. It's about building a relationship, which is tough in that short window of time.

You have to be willing to constantly put yourself out there. A friend of mine had a rule that when he paid for his people to go to the Homebuilder's convention every year, if he caught them having breakfast or lunch with each other he wouldn't pay their expenses. It's very easy to have lunch with your colleagues and strategize about the day, but honestly, just go sit down and find a person in the restaurant that's on their own. Say, "Can I join you?" Could be the best thing you ever do.

I really want to stress to the sponsor's booth people that everybody at an event, including the speakers, are approachable, but you need to approach them in the right way. In other words, you don't go up to someone, even if it's in the booth next door to you, and strike up a conversation when there's potential customers at their booth. You never interrupt someone else that's trying to do business, and you don't try and get a 15 minute consultation with the speaker 10 minutes before he goes on stage. He's got his own ritual to go through. You need to respect that you're there for three days. He's there for an hour and a half. He's really got to bring it. Just say, "I'm going to the airport after you finish speaking. Can I give you a ride?" I've given some real top people rides to airports and made numerous deals. That's one of my favorite things to do... even if my flight doesn't leave until the next day! I even went as far as renting a car just to do that at one event. Bottom line - it was 45 minutes with someone that you couldn't pay $1,000 an hour to talk with privately. Be creative.

There are so many people that will be visiting your booth all day, especially at an event like Traffic and Conversion, one of our primary events, that sometimes it gets hard to talk one-on-one. If your budget allows it, then sponsor a VIP room where you supply snacks and coffee and sodas. You'll have this audience there all day long as well, which is a clever way to do it. Be sure to have one or two associates in the room at all times. Set up appointments to speak with perspective clients that visit your booth. You want to get in front of the people, and then you want to have their attention to build that relationship, to find out more about them and to find out where your product can help them. More importantly...you want to get ahead of the competition.

Attend with an open and abundant mind. I see people who are just totally negative: "The room is hot." "The room is cold." "The coffee's cold." "My feet are killing me." Whatever! Get all that negativity out of your head. It's not serving you. Just look for the opportunity, because it's everywhere and it's in everything.

Don't be the one that the promoter remembers because you bitched about the room or the coffee being late. More than likely they already know about these issues and they're already struggling to take care of them. Don't be remembered as the pain in the ass. Be remembered as someone that was helpful. If you've set up your sponsor booth and have some time to kill before the masses attack, volunteer to help the promoter. The promoters remember that. Invite the promoter and a few of the sponsors out to dinner, or open up your room or suite and have pizza and beers. It's a great way to network, and people will remember you and what you did...on a positive note.

Acknowledge the people that are important to you. Anything you can do to edify them just comes back in spades, and unfortunately too many sponsors are too busy trying to make their numbers. Make the contacts, then the numbers will come.

It's all about relationship building. We're in this for the long term, not just for the three day event. You've got to remember that. Your goal is to form relationships where people will take your calls when you contact them later. And if you're lucky, you'll be personally asked to come back as a sponsor at the next event.

About Sheila Farragher-Gemma

Sheila Farragher-Gemma moved to the states in 1989 for a job in Boston. She figured she would stay a few years before returning home to Ireland, but 25 years later, with a husband, two children, and a handful of successful businesses under her belt, she may be here to stay.

Sheila has an entrepreneurial spirit which lead her to the world of marketing consulting. She loves studying business - watching and understanding what professionals do, and why they do it. Some of her successful business ventures include Scalliwags, a children's indoor playground and much sought after birthday party venue, Foreclosuresmass.com and Government Deal Funding – both Real Estate Investing education companies and Affiliate Mastermind Group - an association bringing structure, innovation and collaboration to businesses in need.

Sheila, through her company Connected Sponsor, helps event promoters monetize their events by building long standing relationships and partnerships with Sponsoring companies. Some events she promotes are Traffic and Conversion, Local Business Summit, Boom Social, Genius Network and Big, Grow, Scale Live.

Her keys to success are tenacity and empathy. Once she gets her teeth into something she doesn't let go. Her dream is to own a business that is so powerful it can run on auto pilot. Think Facebook. She also dreams of traveling to Asia.

When Sheila was young, she was in an equestrian accident while show jumping, and attempting to impress a boy. Her leg was crushed in the fall, but she still loves horseback riding. This so reflects her spirt. She also loves music - her favorite band is Pink Floyd. One thing you might not know about Sheila is she has never eaten a hot dog and never plans to!

To learn how Sheila can help promote your next event, contact her at **sheilagemma@gmail.com.**

> "Most of the important things in the world have been accomplished by people who have kept on trying when there seemed to be no hope at all."
>
> ~Dale Carnegie~

Chapter 12

Become A Branded Expert and Show Your AUTHORity

By Carolyn Lewis

In today's marketplace you need to be THE expert in your field. It's imperative that the public knows, likes and trusts you. So what's the best way to get potential clients to come on board with you? Through Branding.

Your brand is communicated through everything you do – from your name to your logo and slogan to your design theme. Whatever you use to promote a product or service is part of your branding.

Everything your company does is communicated through your brand. It illustrates just who you are and exactly what you do, shows your worth, and distances you from your competitors.

But before you can truly convey your brand, you need to know how your company is perceived by your adoring public. How do they really see you? Do they see you as arrogant or aggressive? Are you approachable, modest and humble? Or are they so confused that they just don't know who you are?

Keep in mind that a brand is not a tangible item. It doesn't exist in our world. So why is branding so important? Because it exists in our customer's minds. Just put yourself in their shoes. When you go looking for a company to do business with, how do you choose? Do you like their logo? Do you like what they have to say on their website? Do you check out their reviews first? How do you first feel about them? Why do you want to buy from them and not their competitor?

For many, many years my mother always wanted to own a Lincoln. Why? It was perceived as luxury. Wealth. It meant that you made it in the world. You were somebody. So why did she feel a Lincoln was better than a Cadillac? Perception. Television commercials showed the cars outside of million dollar homes, at the fanciest restaurants, at the Met. When you went to their showroom it was glamourous and pristine and "smelled like money." So are Lincoln's better? My mom thought so.

Just like with the Lincoln, in order for good branding to work you have to have Perception, Consistency, and Attitude. These are qualities that endear people to you. They want the exact same message every single time they come in contact with your website, with your social media pages, with your brick and mortar storefront, and with you. Don't be funny and whimsical on Twitter, and then gruff and solemn on Facebook. Your customers won't know who you are, so they won't want to do business with you. A seamless user experience is what they want, and that is why they will choose you.

Credibility

Branding comes in all forms, and credibility is a huge part of the equation. Before people learn to trust you, you have to be credible. Before you can create credibility as an expert, you have to understand what it is and what isn't.

Let's say you're a blogger and post that it's only a 6 hour flight to New Zealand from Texas, or in Florida it never gets below 79 degrees. Both are false statements, therefore your credibility is gone.

I know I might ruffle a few feathers here, but I just don't understand how a twenty-one year old can call themselves a Life Coach. They haven't even experienced life yet! They haven't been out in the world long enough to know what business is, what works, what doesn't work, and more importantly, who they are. Unless you're one of the rare few who've been extremely privileged, I don't feel you have anything to offer me.

But a forty year old who's been around the block a few times, worked in the business, had or has a few successful businesses of their own, has a good following and is well-known with positive results, this is the type of person that I deem credible.

Here are a few ways to make yourself credible, while branding your business:

1. **Be Professional**
   - Always focus on your client or customer
   - Pay attention to details
   - Always look for a way to take things one step further
2. **Create a Social Media Page**
   - Become a part of your fans' everyday life
   - Answer simple customer service questions
   - This will build confidence in you for potential customers
3. **Create a Membership Your Site**
   - This will demonstrate your expertise
   - Anticipate & deal with issues you've come across in your professional life
   - Reassure your customers that you know what they need
4. **Provide Contact Information**
   - Prove you're a real person
   - Make sure all information can be verified
   - Avoid using PO box numbers
   - Provide a phone number & Skype handle
   - Provide more than one way to contact you
5. **Give Yourself the Mom Test**
   - Would your mother approve of what you're saying on your website?
   - Would your mom recognize your voice in your website content?
6. **Gather Recommendations from Industry Peers & Fellow Experts**
   - Make sure the endorsement is relevant to your audience

7. **Give A Gift**
   - Can be a free gift or a 'lite' version of your product
   - Your gift should leave people wanting to do business with you
8. **Invest in Quality**
   - Every part of your business should project professionalism & quality
9. **Dig into Your Past for Expert Connections**
   - Many people are flattered that you remembered them & want their endorsement
10. **Show Photos on Your Website**
    - Helps people get to know you before they even meet you
    - Offers proof to your potential customers
11. **Network**
    - Meet people in person at conferences, workshops, community events & mastermind retreats
    - Talk with the speakers, the emcee and the host
12. **Be Positive**
    - Come up with solutions for bad conditions
    - Show people how you handle pressure positively
    - Don't complain on social media
13. **Dare to Share**
    - Provide valuable information people can use immediately
14. **Become a Published Author**
    - Produce a top-quality, professional manuscript correctly formatted & thoroughly proofed

Please remember that you don't have to do backflips to establish your branded credibility. Just be *professional, authentic and client focused.*

Show Your AUTHORity

Books have always been a guilty pleasure for me. I remember hiding under the covers with my flashlight trying to finish my book before I could fall asleep. It was in High School (so many years ago!) that the power of the printed word really hit me. I still remember the day we had an actual published author come to our English class. I'll never forget sitting there, just mesmerized while she read to us and told us how she got started writing, how she writes, the many doors it opened up to her, and the messages she could relay through her printed word. Now, I used to write articles for our school and local newspapers, so I understood some of what she was saying. But even though I was writing, somehow it just didn't seem as significant as having a published book.

Jump forward a few decades later. With every book I read, the power of what is printed on a single sheet of paper never ceases to amaze me. Whether it's a fluffy Harlequin Romance, or a J.D. Robb who-done-it, a 'tongue in cheek' from Janet Evanovich, or business acumen from Michael Gerber, I am still left awed and inspired.

For hundreds of years authors have been regarded with respect and admiration – Tolstoy, Nietzsche, Dickens. So it's no wonder that today many entrepreneurs and speakers are published authors.

Do you see the major word that stands out when you see the word "authority?" AUTHOR! By becoming an author, one automatically claims their authority on the subject printed.

Being an author is the definitive demarcation line of attack, as it truly separates you from the pack. Believe it or not, most authors do not write their books for the money. There really is very little money in books, unless you are a J.K. Rowling or a Donald Trump. In the real world of book writing, the actual purpose isn't the book. It's all about what the book will *do for you*. It's all about the new opportunities that will be created, as well as all the doors that will finally open for you.

Becoming a published author will afford you:

- New-found respect and admiration
- Personal satisfaction
- Enhanced credibility
- Expert status with your customers
- New customer surge due to your increased credibility
- Businesses, opportunities, and people naturally seek you
- A high sense of accomplishment
- Newfound connections and increased earnings

Credibility and esteem are what give authors an inside edge. This is an invaluable tool, which used properly, can translate into $$$. When your customers trust their source, it makes it possible for them to make important decisions in their business.

The trust and authority granted to authors is already formed in the minds of the public. This knowledge is worth more than a king's ransom! This knowledge should be the foremost reason for becoming an author. It's all about the new opportunities, the previously closed doors opening, and the enhanced business relationships that being an author create. All this answers the question of:

"Why should I become a published author?"

Think about it. Would you rather work with an "Average Joe," or an "Author/Expert?" Of course you'd rather do business with the expert. So would the majority of the population. Writing a book will allow you to STAND OUT from your competition....and put you at the level of all the other leaders that you have admired.

The bottom line is that being an author automatically makes you a branded expert. If you want an enormous advantage over your competitors....then become a published author and brand yourself as the business expert in your niche.

There is no greater branding, or client enticement, than being a published author.

Whether you decide to write your own book, use a ghostwriter, or be included in a Multi Author book with other leaders, there's no better way for you to create yourself as an authority. Once your potential customers realize that you are a published expert, they will be ready to work with you, while also referring you to others.

Being an author can multiply your chances of getting every customer you meet as a client. You'll profit from being an author for your entire life......

And no one can ever take that away from you.

Here's to taking the next step to becoming the published AUTHORity in your field!

There is no greater branding, or client enticement, than being a published author.

About Carolyn Lewis

The Book Diva

CAROLYN LEWIS knew many years ago the power of the printed word. From writing articles for her local newspaper, to becoming Sr. Editor, to doing interviews for a local radio station, she got an early start into the publishing world.

For many years Carolyn was perfecting her business background in the corporate world, which ultimately led to owning and operating her own businesses, in addition to overseeing her husband's $100 million Land Development business as Chief Financial Officer.

After a diligent review of new business opportunities, the potential to impact people's lives with a published book was by far the next exciting choice. With a true passion and desire for helping entrepreneurs to "take it to the next level," Carolyn is here to assist you in producing your printed book, thereby accomplishing your goal to become the expert in your field.

Carolyn is the co-owner and Managing Editor of Branded Expert Publishing, the #1 Ghost Publishing Company. Even though they are based in the US, they have published authors worldwide, including The UK, Belgium, Africa, Thailand, Australia, Canada, Singapore and Spain, just to name a few.

For information on how you, too, can become the branded expert in your field through the power of becoming a published author, check out her website at **www.brandedexpertpublishing.com,** or contact her directly at **carolyn@brandedexperts.com.**

> *"Courage is being scared to death, but saddling up anyway."*
>
> *~John Wayne~*

Chapter 13

Membership Has Its Privileges

By C. Mike Lewis

Welcome to the **CXOMarketingAcademy.com** E-Learning Marketing System. I want to show you a revolutionary new program specifically designed to help every small business owner instantly generate more leads and make more money for their business.

As a small business owner, it's finally time you stop trading your time for dollars. This Guided Tour reveals a powerful, fully-automated marketing and business growth system that will take any business to the next level.

And best of all, this entire system will be yours, completely branded to you with your picture, your name and your company name. You will then begin to enroll other business owners desperate for both online and offline marketing help into your system... and begin to generate a passive income stream that continues to build in value month to month and can be sold as an asset whenever you elect to sell it.

This system was developed over a 5 year period at a cost of more than $2 million dollars. Experts are calling it the most powerful lead generation and client attraction program ever created.

But don't take our word for it... see for yourself. We'll show you the impressive array of tools, templates, resources, strategies, tactics and live support that will instantly position you as the market leader. I promise you have never seen anything like this before.

When you acquire your own E-Learning Membership Site, you need to fully understand exactly what it is you have at your fingertips.

You now have at your command what many of today's top business growth experts are calling the most powerful lead generation, client attraction and revenue- generating program available anywhere today.

You have complete and total access to all the tools, resources, strategies, tactics, templates and done-for-you marketing that will enable ANY small business owner to out-think, out-market and out-sell their competition... and to literally dominate their market. Let's look at a few of these:

52 Weekly E-classes delivered each week to only the wise and profitable! 'Our Proven 5 Step Formula' brings you a complete E-Lesson each and every week for you to "clone" and make your own - Including many success stories we get emailed constantly... and we have some DOOZIES lined up. Expect your weekly cutting-edge eLearning system to provide you and your business quality education, resources, tools and templates to get and stay on top **while CRUSHING the competition!**

30 Hours of High-End un-cut and uncensored Video from the most powerful marketing minds on the planet (presently!)! Videos Include; 7 Figure Internet Code, How to Get $1,000,000.00 of FREE Publicity, 101 Low Cost No Cost Lead Generation Techniques, Killer Copywriting and Persuasive Marketing Tools, How to get Published and Virtually Guarantee a Best Seller, Selling from the Platform, Effortless Wealth, How to Smash through Mental Roadblocks to Success, and much more. Speakers and resource material contributors include business and marketing legends; **Jay Abraham, Michael Gerber, Rich Schefren, Robert Kiyosaki, Donald Trump, Mike Filsaime, Armand Morin, Paul Hartunian, Joel Bauer, John Childers, Ali Brown, Paul Blackburn, Bill Gates, Jack Welch** and many others.

Our '5 Step Proven Profit Formula' explained, in detail, via 5 hours of pre-recorded live audio in a seminar. **Over 100 ways to profit listed and explained in mouth-watering detail... and it is all yours with your TEST DRIVE!**

'Our 13 Proven Steps to Marketing Success'. Un-cut, un-censored via video in an 8 hour, step-by-step Marketing Workshop. Material includes the most successful Unique Selling Propositions of all time and how you, too, can use them to Jack-UP your Marketing ROI.

Ultra-Detailed training videos which will reveal why you must have an online presence and will guide you through the process of developing or strengthening one. Key topics include: **Twitter, Facebook, YouTube,** Social Networking and Social Bookmarking.

Shockingly detailed and broken-down sales and marketing strategies which will **guarantee an amazing increase in your ability to close a sale.** Includes **step-by-step instructional videos** will give you an excellent understanding of the **fundamentals of internet marketing for your business.**

An 8-part in-depth training series in which you'll discover the concepts and strategies which are the core of any **responsive email marketing campaign.** This series focuses on **how to get your emails read** and how to get your readers to take immediate action.

Product Creation for Small Business Owners - Constant innovation and product creation is the core of any entrepreneur. We show you how to create your own online information product as well as **how to outsource** the job to qualified freelancers.

Over 40 documents and resources which are **critical to the success of any online or offline business.** Some topics include: **Generating Online Traffic,** Creating a Press Release, Building a Joint Venture Army, **Social Media,** Website Creation, **Google Adwords,** Product Launches, plus MUCH MORE!

Your E-Learning System can be used as a fully automated, hands-free system that will provide complete online coaching without you having to lift a finger or physically participate yourself (if you so desire).

You also have the ability to offer weekly Group Coaching which we provide on your behalf. The average Group Coaching Program today averages $500 per month, and you have the option of charging that amount for those you choose to grant access to... or you may offer it as an educational "grant" where you elect to forgo your monthly fee in favor of helping the small business owners you work with.

I'm often asked how I would go about signing up new members myself if I elected to operate my own E-Learning System. Let me be perfectly clear right from the start. The LAST thing I would do if I were looking to generate cash flow quickly would be to focus on signing up new $97 members to my site.

As a coach, I want high dollar coaching clients. I would set up a 4 tier coaching system that would look something like this (adjust to suit your style, strengths and abilities)...

Note; we call the programs on the following pages 'marketing programs' because this is 'the conversation going on inside the business owners head. "I need help with my marketing and someone to show me how to make my phone ring." Marketing is MUCH more powerful to say than 'coaching'. Business owners don't go to bed at night telling their spouse "I desperately need some coaching." Marketing converts better on average. This is your call and feel free to use the word coaching if it makes you feel more comfortable.

Platinum Marketing Program - $48,000 per year ($4000 per month)
Meet with client for one hour 3x per week and provide complete guidance and support

Clients receive access to my online E-Learning System under my personal direction

Diamond Marketing Program - $24,000 per year ($2000 per month)

Meet with client for one hour per week and provide complete guidance and support

Clients receive access to my online E-Learning System under my personal direction

Gold Marketing Program - $12,000 per year ($1000 per month)

Meet with client for one hour every two weeks and provide complete guidance and support

Clients receive access to my online E-Learning System under my personal direction

Silver Coaching Program - $6,000 per year ($500 per month)

Group coaching call each week where clients can ask questions openly and email you for help. Pair up clients in a 'buddy system' and they hold themselves accountable.

Clients receive access to my online E-Learning System

(Note: we used Coaching in the title description for this program as it better reflects the actual deliverables)

My goal would be to leverage all the tools, resources and support within my E-Learning system to enable me to deliver a world-class coaching experience to my clients so they would pay, stay and refer for years to come.

So why do we have your E-Learning System set up to accept monthly members? Because here's the reality that EVERY coach faces. Like it or not, 8 out of every 10 prospective coaching clients you speak with simply can't afford your coaching services... even your lowest tier program.

But these broke small business owners will accept a low cost do-it-yourself alternative program such as your online system. You should be setting up a sales process that generates a flood of prospective serious small business owners who truly want help and guidance to generate more leads and make more money.

Once you attract them, your goal should be to convince them to enroll in your high dollar, top tier marketing program ($48k per year). If you determine they simply can't afford that, based on your assessment of their business and their current financial condition, you then attempt to downsell them into one of your remaining marketing packages ($24k, $12k or $6k).

When you determine that is also not a viable option, THEN you complete the downsell strategy by offering to provide them with total access to your $48,000 top tier coaching program... ONLINE... in a DO-IT-YOURSELF format... for $97 per month (or $1,000 for 12 months).

Think about this! You're offering access to the exact same information you will provide to clients paying you almost $50k per year for the price of a daily cup of coffee. And if that alone isn't enough to compel them to sign up on the spot, then at your option, you can offer them a $5,000 annual educational Grant they can apply to gain total access to your weekly Group Coaching webinars.

In total, they receive a proven and tested, world-class business growth and marketing program worth close to $8,400 annually for $97 per month (or $1,000 for 12 months). You now have the ability to offer your prospects the greatest bargain in the small business market.

The 80/20 rule is a fact of life. Focus on signing new clients for your higher dollar coaching programs. When you learn how to properly position the resources in your E-Learning System to prospective small business owners based on your initial assessment of their business, the prospects that want your top tier coaching programs will surface on their own.

But you will begin to stock your E-Learning System with monthly members through the natural selection process that occurs in speaking with a large number of small business owners... and discovering the ones that are severely challenged financially.

Rule of thumb - for every 20 business owners you speak with, you will typically sign up one new $24,000 annual client... one new $12,000 annual client... and 3 new $6,000 annual clients. Generally speaking, you can expect to acquire one new $48,000 annual client after speaking with 50 business owners, so it really is a numbers game you're playing.

But consider this very realistic breakdown. When you speak with 50 small business owners, you will typically acquire one $48k client... two or three $24k clients... two or three $12k clients.... and 6 new $6k clients. But out of the remaining 38 or so prospects that couldn't afford any of your private coaching services, you should easily enroll 24 of them into your monthly membership program at $97 per month... (or $1,000 for 12 months).

Please note: Your results WILL vary, you may make more or you may not make any money, the actual results are up to you.

But consider this. From my own personal experience, you will consistently discover that 20% to 35% of your monthly members will eventually raise their hand and request to move into one of your high dollar programs. So the more monthly members you enroll, the greater you grow your future private coaching practice.

If you continue to aggressively pursue a systematic lead generation strategy for your coaching practice, you can see that your monthly membership program will quickly overtake the revenue you produce through your private coaching practice.

There's an old saying... "the proof is in the pudding." We couldn't agree more. When you have a system as powerful as the one we offer, and you're confident of its ability to generate more leads and make ANY small business owner more money, then why not prove it right up front... and do so BEFORE you ask the prospect to invest in your program?

Our sideway sales letter consists of 10 free mini-videos... each designed to highlight one specific money making strategy or tactic specifically designed to make any small business owner who applies this information a minimum of $10,000 within just a 30 day period. We literally have the ability to "self-fund" any serious small business owner by making them 100 times more money than we ask them to invest with us from the start.

Who else is doing that these days? The answer... NO ONE! We wanted our members to have a fool proof way to sell their memberships to their sites without having to actually sell. The sideways sales letter does exactly that.

Imagine the power you now have when you can offer a free 30 day trial with 10 free mini-videos that will produce a minimum of $10,000 in those 30 days... and afterward your prospects can continue as a member for just $97 per month?

This is just one more tool in your arsenal to add more and more members to your site and continue to build your monthly income stream to record levels.

You have what many of today's top business experts are calling the single, most powerful lead generation, client attraction and revenue-generating online coaching program available anywhere today. Learn the power of the system we have handed to you... and use it to generate all the new CXOMarketingAcademy.com E-Learning System members you can handle.

P.S. Please remember that at any time you feel ready and qualified to move forward and acquire the professional help that can enable you to build the business of your dreams, visit **CXOMarketingAcademy.com** and check out our E-Learning Marketing System™. It's helping small business owners just like you get the answers and the help they need to build the business they have always wanted.

We created the E-Learning Marketing System™ with the perfect combination of online resources, tools and support to get you out of any financial distress you're presently experiencing... help you get laser-focused on your highest income-producing activities... and help you develop and then apply the fundamentals that build multimillion dollar businesses. Go to **CXOMarketingAcademy.com** to see for yourself.

About C. Mike Lewis

"The Book Guy"

C. Mike Lewis has over 35 years of experience in marketing, finance, construction and real estate. He previously owned and operated several companies in the southeast, including a $100 million land development company.

He is the co-owner of Branded Expert Publishing, the top Ghost Publishing firm in the world, specializing in books, tools and resources for entrepreneurship and small businesses.

His products are practical, hands-on, and based on the real-world experiences of successful entrepreneurs, CEOs, investors, lenders, and seasoned business experts.

Mike's passion for turning non-writers into authors of printed books, with virtually no writing on their part, positively impacts and changes lives.

Using his complete "Done For You" publishing service has helped raise his client-author's authority and recognition in all phases of their businesses.

For more on how Mike can help you, contact him directly at **mike@brandedexperts.com**.

If you would like more information on how you, too, can become a Branded Expert Published Author, or how you can do a Group Book for your tribe, go to

BrandedExpertPublishing.com

or contact:

Mike Lewis

"The Book Guy"

mike@brandedexperts.com

404-281-6552

Carolyn Lewis

"The Book Diva"

Carolyn@brandedexperts.com

404-312-0326